Studying for your Social Work Apprenticeship

Studying for your Social Work Apprenticeship

A Supportive Guide

**Edited by
Laura James**

BLOOMSBURY ACADEMIC
LONDON • NEW YORK • OXFORD • NEW DELHI • SYDNEY

BLOOMSBURY ACADEMIC
Bloomsbury Publishing Plc, 50 Bedford Square, London, WC1B 3DP, UK
Bloomsbury Publishing Inc, 1359 Broadway, New York, NY 10018, USA
Bloomsbury Publishing Ireland, 29 Earlsfort Terrace, Dublin 2, D02 AY28, Ireland

BLOOMSBURY, BLOOMSBURY ACADEMIC and the Diana logo are trademarks of
Bloomsbury Publishing Plc

First published in Great Britain 2026

Cover design: Terry Woodley
Cover image © Sixteen Miles Out/Unsplash

Bloomsbury Publishing Plc does not have any control over, or responsibility for, any third-
party websites referred to or in this book. All internet addresses given in this book were
correct at the time of going to press. The author and publisher regret any inconvenience
caused if addresses have changed or sites have ceased to exist, but can accept no
responsibility for any such changes.

A catalogue record for this book is available from the British Library.

A catalog record for this book is available from the Library of Congress.

ISBN: HB: 978-1-3505-2764-5
PB: 978-1-3505-2763-8
ePDF: 978-1-3505-2766-9
eBook: 978-1-3505-2765-2

Typeset by Deanta Global Publishing Services, Chennai, India

For product safety related questions contact productsafety@bloomsbury.com.

To find out more about our authors and books visit www.bloomsbury.com
and sign up for our newsletters.

Contents

About the authors vii

1   **Introduction** *Laura James* 1

2   **Starting your journey as a social work apprentice** *Chris Elliott, Jo Dillon and Laura James* 15

3   **Applying the social work apprenticeship standard** *Gemma Hunt* 37

4   **Applying knowledge and theory to practice** *Jordan Savage and Laura James* 59

5   **Safeguarding and ethical practice** *Laura James and Gemma Hunt* 81

6   **Work-based learning: How to get the most out of workplace opportunities** *Ian Browne and Laura James* 101

7   **Developing as a reflective practitioner** *Mechelle Coulton and Cheryl Lovell* 127

8   Critical thinking for social work practice *Mary Gibson* 153

9   Managing your well-being as a social work apprentice *Laura James* 183

10 Conclusion *Laura James* 201

Glossary 211
Appendices 213
Index 220

About the authors

Ian Browne is a registered social worker and Senior Social Work Lecturer at the University of Chester. Ian is the placement lead for the Social Work Masters and Apprenticeship Programme. His role is predominantly focused on practice and skills development. Prior to this, Ian worked in child protection social work in several Local Authority Child Protection teams. Ian is a qualified practice educator, assessing student social workers since 2015 and is also vastly experienced in both assessing and supporting newly qualified social workers. Ian's research interests focus on the experience of student / apprentice social workers and their practice learning experience.

Mechelle Coulton is a registered social worker and practice educator who has worked for the University of Lancashire since 2020 as an apprentice educator on the social work degree apprenticeship. Prior to joining the University of Lancashire, Mechelle worked within the Adult Services sector and has experience in Older People Services, Hospital Social Work, Rapid Response and Rehabilitation, as well as Community Teams. Mechelle supports with the recruitment and onboarding of new apprentices and supports learners to link the knowledge gained from university within their practice. Mechelle has recently achieved her Associate Fellowship in Higher Education.

Dr Jo Dillon is a registered social worker and head of the Social Work division at the University of Chester. Interested in child participation, her research, knowledge exchange and impact studies focus on how children's understanding about the role of social workers in their lives can be improved, and how children can influence the actions taken on their behalf and services provided for them. Using creative methods, Jo encourages social workers, child protection chairs, IROs, managers and students to design bespoke and unique resources to meaningfully embed participation in child and family social work.

Chris Elliott is a registered social worker and is programme lead of the social work degree apprenticeship at the University of Chester. Chris qualified as a social worker in 2008 and practiced for many years as a social worker, team manager and Court Guardian with children and families. Chris is passionate about challenging oppressive practice and works collaboratively with lived-experience colleagues in recruitment, assessment and education of social work students. Chris is a strong advocate of the social work apprenticeship route.

Mary Gibson is a registered social worker with over fifteen years of experience working in a local authority in adult social care. Mary has been a Practice Educator since 2015 and continues to work as an offsite practice educator with a range of agencies. Mary has worked closely with social work apprentices since 2019 and is currently a lecturer on social work apprenticeship programmes. Mary's interest areas are work-based learning and practice education, person-centred theory and practice, spirituality in social work and social work in adult social care.

Gemma Hunt is a registered social worker and practice educator with a background in Child Protection and Youth Justice. Until recently, Gemma worked at the University of Warwick as Assistant Professor – where she was Year 3 lead on the apprenticeship programme. Gemma has worked within the apprenticeship sector for the past six years and sits on the National Trailblazer Group as well as other national forums. She is an external examiner for two apprenticeship programmes and is often asked to support validation events. Gemma has recently joined University College Birmingham as Head of Department to develop and lead new social work provision.

Laura James is a registered social worker who works as a senior lecturer and course leader for a large successful social work apprenticeship programme at the University of Lancashire. Laura has a background in working with children and families and has been a practice educator since 2014. Laura is an external examiner for the social work apprenticeship programme at another institution and is part of both a national apprenticeship forum and the social worker Trailblazer group. Laura is very interested in the concept of work-based learning and supervision in social work practice and is undertaking some research currently on the impact of supervision in social work as part of her doctoral studies.

Cheryl Lovell is a deputy course leader and apprenticeship educator for the Social Work Degree Apprenticeship at the University of Lancashire. She achieved her master's degree in social work, postgraduate diploma in professional practice and postgraduate certificate in advanced childcare practice at the University of Lancashire. Cheryl is a qualified and registered social worker, with a background in children's safeguarding within a local authority and fostering within an independent fostering agency, latterly specializing in parent and child placements. She is also a stage 2 qualified practice educator.

Jordan Savage is a qualified and registered social worker within the children's Multi Agency Safeguarding Hub (MASH) at Lancashire County Council; he has worked in this role since 2022 following successful completion of the social work degree apprenticeship at the University of Lancashire. Jordan has worked with children and families for fourteen years, spanning the journey of children and families from the inception of referral through to leaving care in supporting roles prior to qualification. Jordan has an interest in research and has engaged in research practitioner roles.

1

Introduction

Laura James

Chapter Outline

The social work landscape in England	2
The social work degree apprenticeship	3
Social Work England	6
Terminology and acknowledgement of difference	7
What to expect from each chapter	9
Finally . . .	13

Welcome, and thank you for choosing to read this book. This book is intended for you as a social work apprentice and seeks to support you throughout your social work apprenticeship journey. The book may also be helpful to those who support you on your apprenticeship journey. Those people who support you will include those such as your training provider, your employers, your workplace mentor and your Practice Educator. The book includes lots of activities, reflective thoughts, ideas, top tips and case studies which aim to support you as an apprentice to extend your learning and development throughout your apprenticeship journey. This book has been written by those who have the knowledge of the social work degree apprenticeship and by those who have experience of supporting social work apprentices. You can expect to see contributions from real social work apprentices, academics who teach and lead on social work apprenticeship programmes and those in social work practice too.

The social work landscape in England

In an ever-changing sector, social work is a profession which seeks to safeguard and provide support to the most vulnerable in society; this is the core principle of the profession. Social work is a challenging job, and those who enter the profession need to have the relevant skills, the passion and a lot of resilience. Social work is a popular aspiration of many individuals seeking a meaningful vocation, and, despite the intensity of the managerial and bureaucratic pressure, individuals like you still strive to join the profession with the intention of making a difference to people's lives. Despite being an aspiration for many, the sector continues to face challenges in relation to both recruitment and retention of social workers. Whilst many people qualify as social workers in England, not all of those who are qualified seek registration or go on to undertake a social worker role. Moreover, a significant proportion of those that do decide to go into social work stay in the profession short term or quite quickly seek other positions, for example, management positions. As a result of such a rapid turnover of social workers (and a somewhat lack of social workers across the country too), a large number of social worker posts are filled by newly qualified social workers, resulting in there being limited experience in the sector. Whilst this is a shared experience for many organizations, it may not necessarily apply to all; however, nationally, it poses an ongoing issue in the sector.

In response to the challenges faced in the sector, the government made funding available to both children's and adults' social work services in 2023 and 2024 respectively in order to support organizations to increase their social worker workforce capacity and to encourage those who may not have the financial resources to pursue social work through the traditional academic route (Gov.uk, 2024). Whilst the impact of this funding cannot yet be evidenced, it is both positive and reassuring that there is a wider recognition of the value of apprenticeships and the need to increase the number of social workers nationally through the apprenticeship route. Whilst the impact of the funding cannot yet evidence a positive impact due to the recency of it, the impact of the social work degree apprenticeship itself is beginning to be recognizably evident due to the rapid growth of the programme across the country and the resilience of social workers who have trained via the apprenticeship route. It is evident that those undertaking the apprenticeship have the potential to qualify as a social worker, and there is a notable difference from an employer perspective in relation to the confidence of those who have qualified through the apprenticeship route; this will largely be because, as an apprentice, you are afforded the very rare opportunity to continuously implement your learning in the workplace, as this is where you will spend most of your apprenticeship.

Whilst relatively still a new concept in the sector, the apprenticeship route into social work, which will be discussed in more detail in the following section, is another route into the profession and, therefore, another social work training option to support the sector to welcome and retain social workers. You will likely have heard of other routes into social work and may have even considered undertaking one; for example, there are undergraduate and postgraduate degree programmes, as well as post-qualifying diplomas and accelerated programmes too. Social work education has evolved over the years, and there are now a number of ways in which individuals can train to be a social worker, making the range of training opportunities available more attractive and accessible to more individuals.

The social work degree apprenticeship

Reflecting on the changes to the apprenticeship standard

Apprenticeships have been around for a long time in England; however, the option of undertaking a degree apprenticeship has only been possible since 2015. Since the introduction of degree apprenticeships, the national interest in it has skyrocketed as apprentices can work, earn and learn at the same time (UCAS, 2023). As well as having a plethora of benefits for the apprentices themselves, degree apprenticeships are an attractive choice for employers, as the apprenticeship model enables employers to develop their employees via a 'grow your own' approach which supports workforce planning and the moulding of social workers for the future. Due to the popularity of the apprenticeship programme, some employers are now recruiting externally too, in order to encourage more people to become social workers through the fully funded route.

Since its approval in 2018 (IfATE, 2023), the social work apprenticeship standard has been adopted by many training providers, and the offer of the apprenticeship in social work has grown significantly on a national level, demonstrating the need and value of the programme within the social work sector. As the apprenticeship programme is another entry route into social work, the introduction of the social work apprenticeship has given training providers and employers a unique opportunity to work together to create a curriculum that meets the needs of the sector. Your training provider will have worked with your organization and others in close proximity to gather intelligence on the challenges faced within the sector, the trends in support needs, the local demographic information and current models of practice being implemented locally. In ascertaining information like this, a curriculum that gives you the knowledge, skills and behaviours required to practise in a contemporary way will have been created. Relationships between training providers and employers are a pivotal part of the success of the apprenticeship, as both need to work together to support apprentices like you through your social work qualification. Uniquely too, the apprenticeship curriculum fully recognizes that you will likely have an abundance of experience and transferable knowledge and skills to bring; this is why your journey will be specifically tailored to you, and you will be stretched and challenged appropriately so that you can be the best social worker you can be.

The social work apprenticeship standard was updated in 2023; some minor revisions were made to the knowledge, skills and behaviours statements, and a collection of social worker occupational duties were added to the standard (see Appendix 1). In 2023, there was also a change made to the End Point Assessment (EPA). The EPA for the social work apprenticeship formerly included further assessment, which has academic credits attached to it; however, the EPA is now a month in duration and does not require you to undertake any further assessment after all of your academic modules have been completed. Instead, the fully integrated EPA now includes the processing of your apprenticeship award at your university's assessment board and the task of sending award details to Social Work England. The development and the changes to the apprenticeship standard will be explored in little more in Chapter 3.

A further positive change that was approved as part of the revisions made to the apprenticeship standard in 2023 was the option for training providers to be able to offer a postgraduate study option. This means that a Level 7 social work academic qualification can be obtained; however, the apprenticeship element will remain as a Level 6, as this is the level at which the apprenticeship standard is approved. Training providers across the country who decide to offer a postgraduate route may do this in different ways; for example, some may offer a postgraduate diploma, and others may offer a full master's degree. This option is likely attractive to those who already have a first degree in another subject. The postgraduate study option also enables employers to gain qualified social workers in less time, which is good news for a sector that continues to struggle with both recruitment and retention challenges. The study arrangements with regard to whether an undergraduate or postgraduate (or both) is available will be dependent upon the arrangements between the training provider and employer (IfATE, 2023). At the point of writing this book, it is worth noting that the Institute for Apprenticeships and Technical Education (IfATE) is transitioning to Skills England and soon the apprenticeship standard information will be accessible via the Skills England website rather than IfATE.

Reflective activity 1.1

If you are at the very beginning of your social work apprenticeship journey (you could be in the application stage or in your first year, for example), it is important that you familiarize yourself with the apprenticeship standard and think about how you are and could be evidencing competency of each knowledge, skill and behaviour.

You can access the most recent version of the apprenticeship standard through this link and will also find it in the appendices (appendix 1)

https://www.instituteforapprenticeships.org/apprenticeship-stand-ards/st0510-v1-1

Task

- Take a look at the set of occupational duties and the knowledge, skills and behaviours which are encompassed within each duty. These are what you will be expected to demonstrate.
- Select three of the duties and then take a look specifically at the knowledge, skills and behaviours associated with each of these.
- How confident do you feel about each statement currently?

- As you move through your apprenticeship journey, what are the experiences that may help you develop further confidence and competence against each of these statements?
- Set three actions and take them to your next session with your workplace mentor.

Social Work England

In 2019, Social Work England took responsibility for the regulation of the profession and the registration of social workers in England. All those who qualify as social workers must apply for registration and cannot practice as a social worker until registration has been granted. Social worker is a protected title in England, and only those on the Social Work England register can call themselves a social worker (Stone and Shannon, 2022).

As the regulator for social work, you, as a social work apprentice, will need to have an in depth understanding of Social Work England's professional standards (Social Work England, 2019). Whilst the standard is aligned to Social Work England as the profession's regulator and whilst it is apparent that the professional standards have influenced a number of the knowledge and skills statements within the apprenticeship standard, there is also an explicit behaviour statement that states apprentice learners must 'adhere to Social Work England's standards of conduct'. This book will frequently refer to Social Work England's professional standards (SWE, 2019), and the topics explored over the course of the book will support you as a social work apprentice to prepare for applying to register with Social Work England. Furthermore, the topics discussed, and the activities included will assist you to think about how you will maintain your professional development post qualification.

It is important to note that at the time of writing this book, Social Work England has begun a revision exercise of its professional standards and is set to implement a set of knowledge, skills and behaviours, which in time will be included in social work programmes 'to enable students and apprentices to develop required behaviours, skills, knowledge and understanding to meet the professional standards'. The newly introduced set of knowledge, skills and behaviours will eventually form the core part of new guidance focusing on 'readiness for professional practice', supporting both the professional standards and Social Work England's education and training standards (Social Work England, 2024). It is crucial to highlight here, in order to prevent any confusion, that the introduction of Social Work England's knowledge, skills and behaviours are separate and different to the social work apprenticeship standards' knowledge, skills and behaviours.

Reflective activity 1.2

Take a look at Social Work England's professional standards. They can be accessed through this link:

https://www.socialworkengland.org.uk/standards/professional-standards/

Firstly, take a look at standard 1: Promote the rights, strengths and well-being of people, families and communities.

Reflect upon the following questions:

- How do you embed each component of standard 1 in your practice currently?
- How can you strengthen how you do this?
- Is there a recent intervention you have undertaken whereby you have implemented many components of this standard? If so, think about how this may constitute as new learning and add this to your off-the-job training record, making reference to Social Work England's standards as well as your apprenticeship knowledge, skills and behaviours.
- Can you identify any gaps? What action is needed?

Now think about the same questions, but for each of the other standards. You could take your reflections to your next session with your workplace mentor.

Terminology and acknowledgement of difference

Whilst the social work apprenticeship standard applies to all who undertake the apprenticeship, the way in which the apprenticeship is delivered will vary significantly across the country. The apprenticeship is a term used for learning that takes place via both on-the-job and off-the-job training.

Each of these concepts will be discussed in much more detail in later chapters. However, to provide some initial context in order to confirm what an apprenticeship consists of, on-the-job training accounts for the hands-on work experience that takes place in the workplace for approximately 80 per cent of your working week as an apprentice; off-the-job training focuses on the new learning that you as an apprentice will acquire through attending university and through further opportunities given in the workplace that align to the development and achievement of the apprenticeship standard. Compared to other methods of social work training, you, as an apprentice studying a social work apprenticeship, will achieve both an academic qualification (an undergraduate Level 6 degree for example) and a Level 6 apprenticeship award.

It is important to note that whilst this book will discuss many examples of practice from the perspectives of a training provider, employer and an apprentice, the experiences of all three will likely be quite different. The needs within the different geographical areas of the sector largely differ because of things like, but not limited to, population demography, funding streams and local needs; these are some of the reasons for why the apprenticeship may be delivered differently, from a workplace position more specifically. As all training providers who deliver the social work degree apprenticeship will need to have their programmes approved by Social Work England, there is consistency in how Social Work England's education and training standards are met; however, there will be very different approaches to how the social work curriculum is designed, and the authors are mindful of this.

Additionally, it is important to acknowledge here that the roles of key people involved in an apprenticeship will differ across the country, and so, for consistency, the terms that will be used to describe key people may be broad at times, for example, employer or organization. Universities or higher education institutions will be referred to as training providers, as this is the correct apprenticeship term. Within training providers, there are often certain people with specific apprenticeship roles who conduct the apprentice progress reviews; for example, the role titles vary within training providers, and so these roles will be referred to as apprenticeship or university tutors, mostly. Finally, the role of the named person within an organization whose job it is to support you as an apprentice from a workplace perspective will be referred to as the workplace mentor.

What to expect from each chapter

A number of different authors have contributed to this book and so each chapter is unique, and the content has been developed by those who have experience of the social work degree apprenticeship in different contexts, as noted earlier on. Each chapter is structured in a similar way in that there will be an introduction to each chapter, recommended reading and reflective activities included. Some chapters will include more supportive exercises that can be undertaken by you as apprentice; these will be topic specific. Chapters will often refer to the apprenticeship standard and Social Work England's professional standards; some chapters will also make reference to BASW's (2018) Professional Capabilities (PCF) framework, as this is relevant to many who are studying a social work programme.

Some chapters will have integrated case studies from real social work apprentices or former social work apprentices. At this point in the introductory chapter, I would like to specifically acknowledge and thank Katie Godwin, Richard Flather and Jordan Savage for giving their time to share case studies that have added a very authentic and hopefully relatable perspective to the contents of some of the chapters.

Any reference made to practice examples will be anonymized, the use of pseudonyms will be used, and case examples may also be largely fictitious (but based on real experiences) in order to ensure the highest degree of confidentiality is maintained. Some of the case studies from social work apprentices will give you first-hand information about how to manage the expectations of the apprenticeship and, most crucially, how to manage your well-being throughout the apprenticeship journey. Each chapter intends to be supportive and written in a way which is accessible to you as an apprentice studying at degree level. As each chapter focuses on a different topic specific to the social work apprenticeship, as a reader, you may decide to dip in and out of different chapters and refer to chapters at different times as a point of reference; conversely, you may find reading the book cover to cover more useful.

Chapter 2 will support you to think about the beginning of your social work apprenticeship journey. It will explore the difference between being a social work apprentice and a social worker; the chapter will also examine the differences between being an apprentice and a social work student, as the differences are vast. In exploring such differences, the chapter seeks to identify the differences in opportunities provided within the sector, acknowledging that employers will provide opportunities and experiences unique to their organizations. In exploring the concept of the employer involvement, this chapter will introduce the role of the workplace mentor and other support mechanisms within the workplace. Moreover, this chapter will consider the professional identity of the social worker role and will examine the expectations of the apprenticeship programme. Finally, this chapter will begin to support you, as social work apprentices, to think about your development against the apprenticeship standard and will support you to begin to analyse gaps in knowledge and skills as you make progress on your apprenticeship journey. The chapter will also touch upon the importance of functional skills and the recent changes, both from an application and End Point Assessment (EPA) requirement perspective and also from an ongoing development perspective.

Chapter 3 focuses on the application of the apprenticeship standard and provides insight into the development of the social work apprenticeship. This chapter unpacks each area of the apprenticeship standard and will give you insight in to how the knowledge, skills and behaviour statements can be developed and enhanced in the workplace and in the classroom. This chapter will provide examples, case studies, top tips and activities that will challenge your thinking as apprentices. Moreover, this chapter will explicitly explore the notion of off-the-job training and will provide some examples of how the development of apprenticeship standard areas can be evidenced as off-the-job. Lastly, this chapter will support you to think about preparing for your End Point Assessment (EPA), acknowledging the national changes to the EPA.

Chapter 4 explores the application of knowledge and theory to practice. Quite often, social work learners view theory and practice as two very separate things; thus, trying to understand how the two fit together can initially be quite challenging. It is crucial that, as an apprentice, you are supported to enhance your knowledge of both theory and other topics and that you have the confidence to put your knowledge into practice within the workplace; this application will further extend your thinking and enable you to have a much greater understanding of the life experiences of those you are working with. This chapter seeks to examine a range of prevalent social work knowledge areas and theoretical notions in context, and, in doing so, there will be examples of how theory has been and can be applied, as well as exercises and top tips to support you as apprentices to extend your thinking and develop the confidence you need to apply your new knowledge in the workplace.

Chapter 5 focuses on the ideologies of safeguarding and ethical practice. As safeguarding is such a big topic, this chapter will consider it from two main perspectives. First, the chapter will support you to think about how you can keep yourself safe as a social work apprentice and will encourage you to think about the knowledge you need to keep yourself safe whilst in the workplace and in the university setting. Second, the chapter will encourage you to think about how you can develop, enhance and embed safeguarding knowledge from a practice perspective. This chapter will examine professional decision-making and will include some topic-specific activities that you can try out and apply to both child and adult social work settings. In exploring these ideas throughout this chapter, consideration will also be given to ethical practice and social work values, and there will be some supportive exercises to support you to think about the application of values and the ethical tensions that may arise during your apprenticeship journey.

Chapter 6 focuses on the work-based learning element of the social work apprenticeship and will support you as a social work apprentice to think about how you can get the most out of the workplace opportunities you are afforded. Each apprentice's journey is very different, and each apprentice is afforded different opportunities within their organization to learn and develop in line with the apprenticeship standard; this chapter will support you to think about how you can shape your own opportunities with support from your employer and training provider. This chapter will emphasize the importance of taking ownership of your own learning journey and will detail the workplace support that should be available to you. This chapter will also explore some of the different approaches to work-based learning and will examine some of the different placement models used within the social work apprenticeship programme across the country. The notion of off-the-job training will be looked at specifically in relation to work-based learning, and the concept of seeking feedback will be explored too.

Chapter 7 will explore the fundamental skill of reflection. Reflection is a crucial part of social work practice. Reflective social workers are able to tune in to their practice and use reflection as a tool to unpack their learning in practice and identify developmental opportunities, which, in turn, improve their practice. This chapter will introduce reflection as key component to social work and will have particular focus on the different types of reflection and the difference between basic descriptive reflection and enhanced critical reflection. The chapter will refer to a number of reflection tools and will include activities to support you as apprentices to understand the importance of refection and to be able to effectively apply critical reflection in practice.

Chapter 8 will support you as a social work apprentice to develop your critical thinking and analysis skills. There is a clear distinction between higher academic grades and evidence of critical thinking; similarly, there is an evidenceable difference in the quality of assessments whereby effective critical analysis has been applied. Critical thinking and critical analysis skills are required and viewed as essential skills in both academia and in the workplace; as a result, this chapter will explore what is meant by critical thinking and critical analysis from both an academic and workplace perspective. In doing so, you will be guided on how to apply the principles examined in your assignments and also within your practice. This chapter will also provide insight into how critical thinking and analysis can be developed and enhanced, as it is appreciated that both concepts can appear quite daunting at first; finally, the chapter will include exercises and top tips to support you to develop both of these crucial skills.

Chapter 9 will focus on the management of your well-being as a social work apprentice. Being a social work apprentice can be very challenging, and trying to find the right balance between work, study and personal life can be difficult, especially at the start of your apprenticeship journey. This chapter will explore the notions of self-awareness and emotional intelligence and will explore the importance of engaging in and getting the most out of supervision. This chapter will explore the support on offer from training providers and organizations and will offer signposting to other useful services and tools. Moreover, this chapter will support you to consider how you can seek support and manage competing priorities that arise during your apprenticeship. This chapter will consider the links between positive well-being and practice and will explore the perception of both stress and imposter syndrome, as these are two things you are likely to experience during your apprenticeship journey. This chapter will share a range of supportive strategies that can help you think about how you effectively manage your time, and there will be a number of activities that you can undertake to increase your self-awareness and further develop your resilience. Finally, this chapter will have two case studies integrated within in, written by two final-year social work apprentices, who have shared their tips on how to manage well-being whilst being an apprentice.

Chapter 10 will summarize and conclude the topics that have been discussed during the other chapters. In doing so, the concluding chapter will highlight the key points that have been shared, and there will be some final top tips included to support you as an apprentice throughout your apprenticeship journey.

Top tip

- As you are working through each chapter, take note of where connections to other chapters are made. This will help you to build and enhance your learning on key topics.

Finally . . .

Being a social work apprentice is both complex and challenging but equally very fulfilling and rewarding (this is what lots of social work apprentices across the country tell us). Finding the balance at the very beginning of the apprenticeship programme as a social work apprentice is one of the most difficult things to overcome due to trying to manage working a full-time job, studying at degree level and having a personal life all at the same time; however, it really does get easier, and, once that initial hurdle of settling in and getting used to the balancing of all of the things you have to juggle has been overcome, the experience is an enjoyable and very worthwhile one. Throughout this book, the challenges for social work apprentices will be explored, and there will be top tips and case studies to support your thinking on both a practical and well-being level. This book seeks to support you, as a social work apprentice, in overcoming this first hurdle and offers support, guidance and knowledge to navigate you (and those who support you) through your whole apprenticeship journey.

We wish you every success in your social work apprenticeship journey and hope you enjoy the book.

To those supporting social work apprentices – thank you for choosing this book, and thank you for supporting the social workers of the future.

Recommended reading

BASW. (2018). Professional capabilities framework. https://new.basw.co.uk/training-cpd/professional-capabilities-framework-pcf.

Social Work England's professional standards (2019). https://www.socialworkengland.org.uk/media/1640/1227_socialworkengland_standards_prof_standards_final-aw.pdf.

Stone, C., & Shannon, M. (2022). *The social work degree apprenticeship*. Critical Publishing.

The social work degree apprenticeship standard. https://www.instituteforapprenticeships.org/apprenticeship-standards/social-worker-integrated-degree-v1-1.

References

BASW. (2018). *Professional capabilities framework*. https://new.basw.co.uk/training-cpd/professional-capabilities-framework-pcf.

Gov.uk. (2024). *Adult social work apprenticeship fund*. https://www.gov.uk/government/publications/adult-social-work-apprenticeship-fund#:~:text=Local%20authorities%20can%20apply%20for,adult%20social%20care%20across%20England.

IfATE. (2023). *Social worker integrated degree*. https://www.instituteforapprenticeships.org/apprenticeship-standards/social-worker-integrated-degree-v1-1.

Social Work England. (2019). *Professional standards*. https://www.socialworkengland.org.uk/media/1640/1227_socialworkengland_standards_prof_standards_final-aw.pdf.

Social Work England. (2024). *Knowledge, skills and behaviours*. https://www.socialworkengland.org.uk/media/vwafnxxu/knowledge-skills-and-behaviours-pdf.pdf.

Stone, C., & Shannon, M. (2022). *The social work degree apprenticeship*. Critical Publishing.

UCAS. (2023). *Why degree apprenticeships are a win-win for students, universities and employers*. https://www.ucas.com/corporate/news-and-key-documents/news/why-degree-apprenticeships-are-win-win-students-universities-and-employers.

2

Starting your journey as a social work apprentice

Chris Elliott, Jo Dillon and Laura James

Chapter Outline

Applying to become a social work apprentice	16
Functional skills	17
Other things to consider when applying and starting your apprenticeship	19
What to expect from the social work apprenticeship	20
How will you be assessed?	22
Professional identity	25
The difference between social work student and social work apprentice	27
Who will support you on your apprenticeship journey?	29
Fundamental British values	31
Chapter summary	33

Your social work journey starts here, and what an interesting and valuable route you have chosen into the profession. The benefits of the social work apprenticeship programme are abundant, significantly in terms of the opportunities for gaining experience, as well as the clear financial advantage due to available apprenticeship funding. Apprentices appreciate the opportunity to meet career goals and personal aspirations, gain further knowledge and skills, and conduct social work specific tasks with people already on their caseload whilst being paid a salary and without accruing university tuition fees (Stone & Worsley, 2022).

This chapter will support you to develop an introductory understanding of the social work apprenticeship and will provide you with practical and reflective activities to support you as you begin your apprenticeship journey. Firstly, it will consider the practicalities of applying for a place on the social work apprenticeship – the qualifications you will need, the importance of functional skills and the recent changes to the requirement of functional skills and the range and depth of your previous practice experience. The chapter explores these things early on, as it might be that you are picking up this book as part of your application preparation.

It will explore the difference between being a learner on the apprenticeship pathway, as opposed to a traditional, full-time social work programme, along with the differences between being a social work apprentice and a qualified social worker. This chapter seeks to identify the differences in learning and practice opportunities provided within the sector, acknowledging that your employers will provide experiences unique to their organizations. The roles of those who will support you during your apprenticeship will be explained, and how these key individuals will work together to assist your progression throughout the programme will be explored. Finally, this chapter will support you to think about embedding British values and functional skills, and will encourage you to think about your development against the apprenticeship standard and will encourage you to begin to analyse the gaps in your knowledge, skills and behaviour.

Applying to become a social work apprentice

The application process for this programme differs significantly from other social work courses due to the way the course is funded, the apprenticeship regulations and specific entry requirements. This section provides a straightforward guide to the application process, although you should expect some variation in process amongst employers and training providers, so it is important that you take time to understand your local requirements.

Crucially, applicants will most likely need to evidence that they have relevant work experience within the social care sector, for example, as a support worker with vulnerable children or adults. Many applicants have vast experience, and this programme provides a unique opportunity for career advancement. A key distinction between this and other social work training programmes is that employers take the lead on selecting and nominating candidates. Individuals cannot apply directly to a training provider for a place on the social work apprenticeship. Local authorities and the NHS are some of the key providers (employers) of social work apprenticeship candidates, and employers will either select internal candidates or advertise externally for social work apprentices.

Employers secure funding for apprentices through the apprenticeship levy, and so as an apprentice, you are not required to pay for your study or contribute to fees. Thus, it is important to consider the expectation that you will remain committed to your employer throughout the duration of the programme. This 'grow your own' approach to gaining qualified social workers benefits employers by assisting with staff retention (Haider, 2024). Candidates also reap the rewards, gaining significant cost-free learning opportunities and qualification whilst retaining their salary.

The initial stage of the application process sits with the employer. Employers use various methods to select their preferred candidates; for example, this may involve an application, written exercise and interview. Once individual employers have selected candidates in whom to invest, they will then liaise with their chosen training provider to commence their selection process. This may feel rigorous and could include submission of an application, a piece of written work, a presentation or an interview, and it might include people who use social work services. In some cases, employers and training providers work together on recruitment and may interview jointly. Ultimately, you should aim to demonstrate your social care experience, adherence to social work values, your academic potential and your commitment to the social work apprenticeship.

Functional skills

Prior to February 2025, having both maths and English at Level 2 or equivalent was a requirement for all apprentice learners; both were needed in order to move through the gateway to the End Point Assessment process (EPA). The Labour government however, in February 2025, announced significant changes in respect of functional skills, and now, for apprentices over the age of nineteen, evidence of maths and English are not a requirement of the gateway process and so are not a barrier to the completion of an apprenticeship. Employers, however, can decide if they wish for their apprentices to evidence or continue to complete functional skills; whilst some employers may opt for functional skills to remain essential to the apprenticeships they facilitate, the completion of functional skills will not be a barrier to moving through the gateway process. It is important to highlight here that each employer across the country make take a different approach, and so ensuring you are clear is vital.

It is also important to note that Social Work England require that training providers assess that those applying for social work training programmes can demonstrate that they have a good command of English. For applicants from the UK, this is typically assessed through evidencing that you have the equivalent of GCSE English at Level C, or 4, or above.

Whilst evidencing completion of functional skills at a certain level has changed, it is crucial to highlight that the application of maths and English still does form a part of apprenticeship delivery, and there will be an expectation that you apply maths and English skills in different ways throughout your apprenticeship studies, both in the classroom and in the workplace. This is something that will be monitored as part of your regular progress reviews and something that will remain subject to wider governance, for example, Ofsted inspection. You may also be asked to complete a short online maths and English diagnostic test to demonstrate your competence in both of these skill areas; this diagnostic assessment will give you an indicator of your current competence level in maths and English and will influence the support needed throughout your apprenticeships, enabling you to apply both skills throughout your apprenticeship studies.

Top tip

- Ask your linked training provider how English is evidenced, and ask your employer about their position of the completion and evidencing of functional skills.

Other things to consider when applying and starting your apprenticeship

It is essential that you demonstrate good health and good character prior to acceptance onto the programme. This is normally evidenced by completion of an Enhanced Criminal Record Disclosure, as well as an occupational health confirmation in some cases. These are standard checks completed by employers. Please note, not all previous convictions exclude people from a social work career; decision-makers will consider needs, strengths and protective factors alongside any risks. There is also a requirement for completion of a self-assessment skill scan which measures the knowledge, skills and behaviours (KSBs) of applicants. This ensures that prospective candidates meet the criteria for the programme and that the course will provide them with sufficient opportunity for new learning, thus benefitting them and their employer. We will take a further look at social work KSBs and skills scans later in this chapter, and they are more deeply unpicked again in Chapter 3.

It is worthy to note here that it is unlikely you will be given a choice about which training provider you complete the programme with. Each employing organization is affiliated to a specific training provider; therefore, it is worth exploring which university is linked to your chosen apprenticeship to ensure it is accessible to you. Whilst the application process may feel overwhelming, your employer and the training provider will support you in gathering and submitting the required evidence. This will no doubt feel worthwhile once you commence the social work apprenticeship programme, as research with social work apprentices found that 'one hundred percent (n = 29) of the respondents reported being pleased that they accepted a place and equally, all said they are enjoying the apprenticeship' (Stone & Worsley, 2022: 682). The collated evidence and self-assessment tasks will result in the creation of a bespoke training plan to ensure you receive the right learning and support during the apprenticeship.

Reflective activity 2.1

How prepared are you to begin your application?

Update your CV, focusing on your work experience in the health and social care sector. Highlight significant and relevant roles and responsibilities.

Spend some time thinking of examples of good practice from your work experience. Write them down, as these will help you when preparing for an interview – for example, a time when you have worked effectively as part of a team.

Write a short statement detailing your strengths, key skills and the areas in which you would like to develop these further. Practice talking about these out loud. This statement will be useful for both your application and your interview.

When thinking about undertaking the social work apprenticeship, what are you most looking forwards to, and what are you most worried about? Write these things down. It might be helpful to talk these through with social workers, colleagues or perhaps the linked training provider. By doing this, some of your worries may be alleviated.

What to expect from the social work apprenticeship

Training providers offering the social work apprenticeship must be approved by Social Work England. Social Work England is the statutory regulator for social work, and social work apprentices must evidence standards of proficiency to apply for registration following qualification (IfATE, 2022). All aspects of the apprenticeship must align with Social Work England's qualifying Education and Training Standards (2021) and their Professional Standards. As a regulated profession, there is both a recognition and appreciation that in order to become a social worker, there must be a period of degree level study, assessed practice and thorough assessment determining suitability for the social worker role.

Now that the social work apprenticeship can be studied through a postgraduate route, the duration of the apprenticeship can vary; the typical undergraduate route usually takes three years to complete. If you work full time, you will usually spend four days in the workplace undertaking on-the-job activities and will typically attend one day each week engaging in new learning through your training provider. An essential component of the apprenticeship programme is the notion of 'new learning'; you will not simply continue in your current role and be released to attend university once per week. Instead, your employer will provide you with new learning opportunities in the workplace to allow you to consolidate your learning from the classroom. The concepts of both on- and off-the-job training are explored in detail in Chapters 3 and 6.

To meet the Social Work England requirements for registration, social work apprentices must complete at least 200 days on placement (which can include up to thirty skills days) throughout the programme (SWE, 2021). These are two distinct and different placements that are undertaken and evidenced during your apprenticeship. Chapter 6 explores the different approaches to placement in more detail. Social Work England's Qualifying Education and Training standards (2021) stipulate that:

> Each student will have placements in at least two practice settings providing contrasting experiences and a minimum of one placement taking place within a statutory setting, providing experience of sufficient numbers of statutory social work tasks involving high risk decision making and legal interventions.
>
> (Social Work England, 2021: 2.1)

Whilst you may have already identified your chosen area of specialism (such as working with children, families or vulnerable adults), it is important to note that the programme is generic. Therefore, on completion and following registration with Social Work England, you will be eligible to practice as a social worker in any social work role within any organization.

Employers are usually responsible for organizing your social work placements, in accordance with the needs of the employer and your areas of interest and learning; in some cases, however, it may be that your training provider has a lead role in organizing your placements. It is very likely that, to achieve the contrasting nature of placements, you will undertake one placement in an area of social work you had not previously considered. There will be elements of the social worker role that you are already familiar with, such as building relationships with children, families and vulnerable adults or utilizing an assessment model to request the provision of services to people with disabilities or learning needs. You may already be working within a hospital, familiar with discharge procedures and paperwork, or supporting children leaving care as personal advisors. With apprentices coming from a wide range of local authorities, NHS trusts or other organizations and being located within different teams and specialisms, your classroom-based learning is enriched by the experiences of others. Do make the most of listening to your peers, learning more about their social work practice and the challenges they face in their daily roles. This is a unique opportunity which is very rewarding.

Studying at degree level alongside full-time work is indeed a challenge, and it is recommended that you take time to consider what support you will need to manage all of these competing demands. Take time to investigate the course prior to commencing; each training provider will have their own website and programme handbook providing you with a plethora of useful information. Take a look at Chapter 9 for tips of how to manage the competing demands, and later on in this chapter, there is an activity which will support you to think about your support network.

Top tips

- Look at the website of your training provider, and ask them for the programme handbook. This will give you more insight into the programme itself but also the different types of support available to you whilst you are studying your social work apprenticeship.
- Ask your employer about how your placements will be organized. This will give you time to think about your learning needs and areas of interest.

How will you be assessed?

Throughout your social work degree apprenticeship journey, you will be continuously assessed. The academic qualification you will do as part of your apprenticeship will carry a certain number of credits. For an undergraduate programme, for example, the three-year programme normally totals 360 credits, equating to 120 credits per each academic year. Throughout the three-year programme, you will complete a variety of modules to support your learning and prepare you for practice. The modules studied will vary across the country; however, as all social work programmes require validation from Social Work England and given the fact that the degree is recognized nationally as a generic one, there will be a degree of similarity.

The academic modules studied will provide you with a depth of understanding of social work, drawing upon relevant legislation, associated research findings, linked statutory guidance and wider reading, all of which will promote application into practice. For example, in year one, you may focus on learning the fundamentals of social work practice through learning about social work law, human growth and development, values and ethics. In year two, you may delve more deeply into specific elements of social work practice, such as social work theory and methods, child and family social work and adult social work. Year three may focus on aspects of critical and radical social work practice before undertaking final modules that draw together all knowledge, skills and behaviours, underpinned with critical analysis, critical reflection, risk assessment and defensible decision-making. All your modules will be enhanced with teaching and collaborative working with people with lived experience of social work services, along with the specialist input of qualified social workers from a variety of backgrounds. Each academic module will include an assessment so that your understanding can be substantiated. The assessment methods used by training providers will again vary; however, these may include written essays, presentations, verbal dialogues, portfolios, reports, poster presentations, role-plays, leaflets, workbooks and examinations.

As well as being assessed in a summative manner, there will be formative assessments undertaken both in the classroom and in the workplace, particularly during placements. Formative assessments ensure a regular and informal approach to assessment, such as group discussions in the classroom, practice reflection and observations of practice. This ensures the provision of feedback throughout, thus supporting your learning regularly. Learning from feedback will be a valuable tool ensuring your progression and development during the programme, as well as throughout your social work career. Chapter 6 looks at learning from feedback in more detail.

In addition to studying the academic modules, you will be assessed in another light in order to demonstrate you are making progress against the social work apprenticeship standard. This again may be done slightly differently; however, through regular progress review meetings with your workplace mentor and named member of staff from your training provider, you will be supported to reflect upon how you are applying classroom learning into practice, and you will be encouraged to think about how your confidence is developing from an apprenticeship standard perspective. Each time you attend a progress review, conversations and examples of practice will be shared and recorded; this provides sound evidence for the progress made outside of the classroom. In addition, as an apprentice, you will be expected to record your off-the-job training regularly in order to demonstrate that you are undertaking enough to achieve full competency against the social work apprenticeship standard. Training providers may use different systems to enable you to record your off-the-job training; however, the principles of recording will be the same, as all training providers are governed by the same apprenticeship funding rules.

Towards the end of your learning journey, after you have completed your academic modules, evidenced progress against the standard and recorded sufficient new learning, you will reach what is known as the gateway period; this is followed by the End Point Assessment. The newly revised, month-long EPA seeks to evidence that you have fully achieved what was set out on your apprenticeship training plan and that you have successfully reached the highest competency level of the apprenticeship standard. During the month-long EPA, a course assessment board takes place through your training provider, whereby your academic award is ratified, and your award details are then shared with Social Work England, enabling you to apply for registration. The EPA was explored in detail in Chapter's 1 and 2. In addition to gaining a degree or postgraduate level certificate from your training provider, you will also receive an apprenticeship certificate.

Reflective thoughts

You have read about the different ways in which you may be assessed during your apprenticeship. Are there any assessment methods that you feel you may need to develop your knowledge and skills of? If you have studied previously, can you recall the feedback you received? What were your strengths? Which assessment methods leave you feeling a little more nervous? What could you do about this?

Take a look at the recommended reading section at the end of this chapter, as some assessment specific texts have been selected. These may be helpful to do as you embark on your academic studies.

Think about the assessment methods discussed that relate to your work-based learning. Write down any thoughts you have on these and arrange to talk to your workplace mentor about these. Do you have any other ideas of how you could be assessed in the workplace? Can you think of any other ways in which you would like to receive feedback on your progress?

Professional identity

After exploring whether you meet the practical requirements to apply for the social work degree apprenticeship, it is vital to recognize the shift from being a social care professional to a social work apprentice. For some, this may be the first journey into the world of higher education, and both your training provider and your employer will support you regarding all aspects of academic writing and classroom-based learning. Due to the nature of the programme, your work-based role may also change, and you are likely to be immersed in new situations and experiences that take you out of your comfort zone. But what is social work, and how will your new learning differ from what you are already doing?

As noted by Thompson (2015; pg. 1), 'some people use the term "social work" to refer to any type of activity that is geared towards helping people solve their problems'; for example, health and education professionals can sometimes infer that they are doing 'social work'. Whilst there is a certain appreciation for the work other professionals do, there is also a real misconception of what social workers actually do and a general misunderstanding of the difference in work of social workers and other helping professions (Thompson, 2015).

Quite often, social worker apprentice learners say that they feel as though they are undertaking the role of a social worker but without the 'piece of paper' that confirms they are a social worker. Whilst this may resonate with you, there are some clear differences that distinguish the roles. It is important to again highlight that the protected title of 'social worker' can only be legally used by those who are suitably qualified and registered with Social Work England. Due to the protected nature of the role, there are elements of social work that, as a social work apprentice, you are unable to carry out alone due to the legal implications, such as statutory visits to children on child protection plans. As a social work apprentice, you will be afforded lots of opportunities to work alongside social workers and will no doubt be undertaking social worker tasks; however, these tasks will be supported, overseen and guided by registered social workers. Stone and Worsley's (2022: 682) research with social work apprentices notes that 'nearly 90% of apprentices have noticed a positive change in their day to day practice with people with lived experience as a result of learning during the apprenticeship course', with even the newest of learners reporting positive change. Regardless of your current level of knowledge and skills, your workplace mentor will help you identify how you can progress, learn and excel in the social work field.

Apprentice workloads are protected and therefore likely to be smaller than those of your colleagues. Whilst you may embrace the change in pace and the wealth of new learning, it may be difficult for your colleagues to understand how your new role differs to your previous role. If you are an internal candidate, for example, who is beginning an apprentice role within your usual team / office, you may find colleagues asking you to assist with duties that belonged to your 'old' role or to meet with people who had previously been on your 'old' workload. Your organization may take time to make the shift also, with computer databases and systems requiring you to process tasks that no longer fit with your apprentice role. In your initial meetings with your workplace mentor, take time to discuss the changes to your roles and ask how these will be communicated to your colleagues and the wider organization.

Alongside the change in your previous role and your new apprentice identity, it will be necessary to think about the changes in relationships that you will have built with those with lived experience. You and your manager / workplace mentor will need to identify whether your work with the family / individual is complete, as your 'relationship is a professional relationship for a professional purpose' (Reimer, 2017: 1360). However, with relationship-based practice being at the heart of social work, it can be difficult to move away from these connections, as you may have known and worked with these people for many years. Do ensure that those you have supported know who their new contact within the organization is, if work is to continue, and that your relationship with them adheres with the BASW Code of Ethics (2021) and in-line with your organizational policies.

To explore the social work role a little further, let's go back to what Thompson (2015) discusses. Above, the statutory role of the social worker was introduced; much of the work of some professionals working in 'helping professions' will be underpinned by legal frameworks. However, social workers have specific statutory duties that 'set them apart from other groups' (Thompson, 2015); for example, social workers investigate abuse in line with the relevant law amongst other duties. As a result of the range of statutory duties a social worker has, they carry legal accountably for the decisions they make. As you progress through your social work apprenticeship journey, you will no doubt be surprised about how closely linked social work is to the legal context. Through having the opportunity to work more closely with social workers and to have the opportunity to undertake some tasks under their guidance and with supervision, you will likely change the perception you had earlier on in the programme about the role of the social worker and how this really differs from other helping professions. Chapter 5 will explore the safeguarding context in detail and will support you to understand more about how social workers work within the law to seek social justice and through examination of care versus control; you will become clearer on the complex decision-making involved in the social worker role, and the ethical tensions that often arise will be explored too.

Reflective activity 2.2

Consider the role you are doing now (or have previously undertaken) and reflect on how this differs from the role of a social worker. What different decisions would social workers need to make? How would their knowledge and skills differ from yours currently? What would you need to learn to become a social worker? If possible, speak to a social worker – ask them about the progression from social care work to the role of being a qualified social worker.

The difference between social work student and social work apprentice

Prior to securing a place on the social work apprenticeship, you may have wondered (and still be wondering) what is unique about being a social work apprentice rather than a social work student. As noted in the introductory chapter, there are many different training routes into social work, and over the decades, there have been changes to the qualification and the curriculum that underpins it. Essentially, if we were to examine the apprenticeship programme compared to other social work programmes, the academic qualification at the end is the same. However, as an apprentice learner, you will also gain an apprenticeship qualification: a Level 6 apprenticeship certificate. You would receive a Level 6 apprenticeship certificate whether you study the Level 6 or Level 7 academic qualification.

The curriculum in relation to the modules you study may also largely be the same or, in some cases, identical to other social work programmes; however, the way in which modules are taught and assessed are often different for apprentice learners. This is because there is recognition that all learners join the apprenticeship with differing levels of experience, and given you are already working in a relevant setting, you will have begun to develop (or may already have years of developing) the people skills needed for social work. Through your interactions with those with lived experience and other social work professionals, you will likely have some experience that can be drawn upon in the classroom.

This chapter (and the following chapter too) has introduced the knowledge, skills and behaviours (KSBs) of the apprenticeship standard; these are fundamental to apprenticeship programmes and are the key qualities that candidates must evidence to demonstrate competence against the standard. The social work apprenticeship KSBs currently comprise of thirty-five knowledge, fifty skills and five behaviour statements essential for the social work profession. For example, 'skill six: Practicing in a non-discriminatory manner', and 'knowledge statement four: How to develop relationships appropriately' (Skills England, 2025) – both of which you may feel a level of competency in at the point of starting your apprenticeship.

Completion of the initial skill scan during the application and onboarding process enables candidates like you to reflect upon and measure their competence in relation to each of the KSBs. Each apprentice is then provided with their own individualized training plan from the training provider. This initial skills scan is an invaluable exercise which 'measures how well the apprentice meets the requirements for knowledge, skills, and behaviour described in the occupational standard. This may be a self-assessment, with a follow-up discussion' (Department for Education, 2023: 6). You are encouraged to be as accurate as possible when reflecting upon your current knowledge and skills as eligibility for the apprenticeship requires measurable progress throughout the programme. The programme will therefore not be suitable for those who are assessed as already fully competent with regards to KSBs. This can be challenging for you when you are presented with the skill scan, as you may feel that you need to score yourself highly in order to gain a place on the apprenticeship, or you may feel that because of the level of experience you have had in your current or previous role, that you are very skilled and knowledgeable in the areas outlined in the KSBs. It is important to think about each KSB statement from a social worker perspective rather than from the perspective of your current role; this will enable you to present a more accurate reflection of your starting point and will also broaden your understanding of the difference between the social worker role and the role you currently have.

Reflective activity 2.3

Take a look at the social work apprenticeship standard and think about how you confident you feel about each knowledge, skill and behaviour statement in your current role. Think about each statement again from a social worker perspective. What differences do you notice?

Who will support you on your apprenticeship journey?

Your employer:

Your work-place mentor

Your line manager

Workforce development team/HR

Practice Educator

You – the social work apprentice

Friends and Family

The training provider:

University tutors

Teaching staff

Programme leaders

Inclusive, well-being and academic study skills support

As a social work apprentice, you will have a team of support around you throughout your journey. Your employer has committed to invest in your apprenticeship training and help you to achieve; therefore, there will be dedicated people in the workplace to guide you. There will be a named person in your organization who will manage the apprenticeship contract side of things; this person usually sits in an HR or workforce development team. They will take responsibility for the practical, financial, administrative and regulatory aspects of the process.

Throughout the programme, you will also have a dedicated workplace mentor. They are usually a registered social worker and will meet with you regularly, providing support and encouragement to apply your new knowledge into practice. It is their role to help you identify learning and training opportunities in the workplace to enable you to enhance your confidence and make progress with achieving and evidencing the knowledge, skills and behaviours (KSBs). Your workplace mentor will provide challenges and will stretch your thinking and learning to ensure you are fulfilling your potential and making good progress. In considering the role of the workplace mentor, it is important that there is distinction between day-to-day case management and mentoring; quite often, the best way to manage this is with separate supervision and mentoring sessions; this means that prior planning is essential. Sometimes, your workplace mentor may be somebody different to your usual manager. Whether your workplace mentor is your manager or another colleague, the relationship you build with them will provide a good foundation for your learning.

In addition to building relationships with academic staff who will teach you during your classroom-based studies, you will have a named person from your training provider whose role is to support you and review your progress frequently throughout your apprenticeship, right up until you reach the gateway point that leads to your End Point Assessment. The names of these individuals vary across training providers. This named person will review your progress frequently throughout your apprenticeship, ensuring compliance in recording new learning, as well as providing general advice and support. They will ensure that you are accessing new learning both on and off the job and will signpost you to all required services available within the education provider setting.

Your employer and education provider will work collaboratively to ensure you are well supported throughout your apprenticeship journey, to encourage your academic and professional development and to address any issues that may arise. This is organized formally through regular progress review meetings that are attended by you, your workplace mentor and your named person from your training provider. KSBs are central to the review process, as you will be expected to provide evidence of progress in relation to the apprenticeship standard. Within the meeting, SMART targets will be set and reviewed to ensure development and stretch. The review process entails vital communication between training providers and employers, thus ensuring information sharing and holistic support for you on your apprenticeship journey. This means that you as the apprentice will feel empowered and receive a personalized plan of support.

Reflective activity 2.4

Whilst this part of the chapter has highlighted the key people, from your employer to training provider, it is important to think about who else may be supporting you outside of these two organizations.

The social work degree apprenticeship is a demanding programme; you are working full-time alongside studying at degree or postgraduate level. Who is supporting you and championing your achievements? How will you protect your own health and well-being? Do consider the support you have in place in the home but also any support you may need from the training provider or, indeed, your employer. Your training provider will have lots of services that are available to you; for example, if you have a learning support need, do you need to access some additional support when writing your assignments? Would you benefit from support with managing your well-being?

Try writing down who else may be a part of your support network during this time. It would be a good idea to talk to them to explain that you will be undertaking an apprenticeship.

Who else will support me?

1. _____
2. _____
3. _____
4. _____
5. _____

Fundamental British values

The concept of Fundamental British values was originally introduced in the *Prevent* strategy; this was a government-issued guidance aimed at responding to the threat and promotion of terrorism in the UK (HM Government, 2011). The British values are:

- Democracy.
- The rule of law.
- Individual liberty.
- Respect for those with different faiths and beliefs.

Prevent stipulates that close attention must be given to people and organizations who offer interventions to vulnerable people, recognizing the influence they have and the need to establish what organizational and personal values they hold (HM Government, 2011). The thinking behind the strategy was that those upholding British values would be unlikely to act in extremist ways, as in, the 'vocal or active opposition to fundamental British values' (HM Government, 2011: 107).

In 2014, the Department for Education, under the Coalition Government, published guidance on actively promoting fundamental British values within both independent and state-maintained schools (Department for Education, 2014). Educational institutions must demonstrate how their policies consider and promote British values, how the values are evident within the curriculum and how they are embedded amongst the school's wider activities and ethos (Revell & Bryan, 2018). Ofsted's (2023: 11) Education Inspection Framework was updated to include British values as part of their inspection criteria, ensuring that:

> The provider prepares learners for life in modern Britain by: equipping them to be responsible, respectful, active citizens who contribute positively to society; developing their understanding of fundamental British values; developing their understanding and appreciation of diversity; celebrating what we have in common and promoting respect for the different protected characteristics as defined in law.

British values underpin the social work degree apprenticeship. Apprentices are encouraged to have confidence in their values, in turn, equipping them to advocate for the rights of the vulnerable, oppressed and persecuted. British values will be discussed and recorded as part of your progress reviews, and you are encouraged to consider how you can apply them in your recording of new learning too. Your classroom-based activities and teaching will present you with a diverse range of learning opportunities, all carefully planned to ensure personal development. Studying modules such as social work law and ethics, for example, will provide you with the knowledge and skills to lobby people and organizations in positions of power, to challenge unfair policies and procedures, and to fight for equality and parity. The Code of Ethics for social workers (BASW, 2021:3) reminds its members to 'act ethically and have the professional rights necessary to protect and promote the rights of people who need to or who access social work services'.

In order to develop your thinking of British values further, considering the value of anti-oppressive practice and associated models that support you to critically think about the impact of oppression and anti-oppressive working will be useful to you. You can find more detail on these things in Chapters 7 and 8.

Reflective activity 2.5

Let's think more deeply about the fundamental British values. Take time to consider each question in relation to your current workplace:

- What does democracy mean?
- Can you identify examples of democracy in your workplace?
- What laws and legislation underpin your current role in health and social care? What services does this legislation enable you to offer to improve the lives of people?
- In social work, individual liberty is upheld wherever possible. What situations, or systems, may affect a person's degree of individual liberty?
- Take time to refresh yourself with the protected characteristics under the Equality Act 2010. Which protected characteristic aligns with one of the above British values?

Chapter summary

This chapter has introduced you to the framework of the social work apprenticeship and provided you with an explanation of what you will need for your application which forms the very first step. Whilst each training provider and employer will follow different admissions processes, academic module choices and assessment methods, the social work apprenticeship programme across England will be similarly structured due to their alignment with Social Work England's qualifying Education and Training Standards (2021). Showing that you are consistently meeting the apprenticeship standard, via the recording of new learning, attendance at progress reviews and progressing through the End Point Assessment, is key, and you will be fully supported in this task by your training provider, workplace mentor and your employer. Finally, this chapter considered professional identity and how this changes as an apprentice and future social worker. The changes to your professional identity will enable you to progress into the social worker role and undertake statutory tasks that can only be completed by qualified and registered social workers.

You have chosen an exciting and challenging route to become a social worker, and we wish you all the very best in starting your apprenticeship journey. Chapter 3 will now focus more deeply on the application of the apprenticeship standard and facilitating your ability to develop and enhance your knowledge, skills and behaviour within both the workplace and the classroom. It will also unpick the requirement of 'off the job' training whilst supporting you to think about how you can prepare for your End Point Assessment.

Recommended reading

BASW. (2021). *The BASW code of ethics for social work*. https://basw.co.uk/policy-practice/standards/code-ethics.

Cottrell, S. (2024). *The study skills handbook* (6th edn). Macmillan Education, Limited.

HM Government. (1998). *Human rights act*. https://www.equalityhumanrights.com/human-rights/human-rights-act (accessed 19 January 25).

HM Government. (2010). *Equality act*. https://www.equalityhumanrights.com/equality/equality-act-2010.

McMillan, D. K., & Weyers, D. J. (2021). *The study skills book* (4th edn). Pearson Education.

Social Work England. (2021). *Education and training standards*. https://www.socialworkengland.org.uk/standards/qualifying-education-and-training-standards-guidance-2021/.

References

BASW. (2021). *The BASW code of ethics for social work*. https://basw.co.uk/policy-practice/standards/code-ethics (accessed 19 January 2025).

Department for Education. (2014). *Promoting fundamental British values as part of SMSC in schools*. https://assets.publishing.service.gov.uk/media /5a758c9540f0b6397f35f469/SMSC_Guidance_Maintained_Schools.pdf (accessed 19 January 2025).

Department for Education. (2023). *Apprenticeships: Initial assessment to recognise prior learning*. https://www.gov.uk/government/publications /apprenticeships-recognition-of-prior-learning/apprenticeships-initial -assessment-to-recognise-prior-learning (accessed 19 January 2025).

Haider, S. (2024). Promoting diversity in social work education in England through work-based route. In R. Baikady & J. Przeperski (Eds.), *The Oxford handbook of power, politics and social work* (pp. 318–34). Oxford University Press.

HM Government. (1998). *Human rights act*. Crown.

HM Government. (2010). *The equality act*. Crown.

HM Government. (2011). *Prevent strategy*. https://www.gov.uk/government/ publications/prevent-strategy-2011 (accessed 19 January 25).

Institute for Apprentices and Technical Education. (2022). *End-point assessment plan for social worker statutory integrated degree apprenticeship*. Crown.

Ofsted. (2023). *Education inspection framework*. https://www.gov.uk/ government/publications/education-inspection-framework/education -inspection-framework-for-september-2023 (accessed 19 January 25).

Reimer, E. C. (2017). Leaving the door open for "tune ups": Challenging notions of ending working relationships in family work. *Child & Family Social Work, 22*(4), 1357–64.

Revell, L., & Bryan, H. (Eds.). (2018). *Fundamental British values in education: Radicalisation, national identity and Britishness*. Emerald Publishing.

Skills England. (2025). *Social worker* (integrated degree). https://skillsengland .education.gov.uk/apprenticeships/st0510-v1-1.

Social Work England. (2021). *Education and training standards*. https://www .socialworkengland.org.uk/standards/qualifying-education-and-training -standards-guidance-2021/ (accessed 19 January 2025).

Stone, C., & Worsley, A. (2022). "It's my time now": The experiences of social work degree apprentices. *Social Work Education, 41*(4), 675–90.

Thompson, N. (2015). *Understanding social work: Preparing for practice*. Palgrave.

United Nations. (1989). *United Nations convention on the rights of the child*. United Nations.

3

Applying the social work apprenticeship standard

Gemma Hunt

Chapter Outline

How has the social work apprenticeship standard developed? 38

The social work degree apprenticeship standard:
   occupation duties 40

The knowledge, skills and behaviour statements 41

Tracking knowledge, skills and behaviours during
   progress reviews 44

How do I evidence the knowledge, skills and behaviours? 45

Off-the-job training 49

What can be included as off-the-job training? 50

The importance of stretch and challenge during the
   apprenticeship 52

What is the End Point Assessment? 55

Chapter summary 55

The Social Work Degree Apprenticeship (SWDA) was initially approved in November 2018, with the first university programmes commencing in 2019 after obtaining approval from Social Work England. The SWDA was introduced as a new pathway into social work, complementing the existing routes on offer, and was seen as an opportunity to invest in the existing workforce – to support existing staff to access training whilst remaining 'on the job'. Although the apprenticeship is often described as an alternative to the existing undergraduate and postgraduate professional training routes, it is mostly the method of delivery that is different. As seen in other apprenticeships, work-based learning is a key aspect of the SWDA, with apprentices spending 80 per cent of their time learning in the workplace. The remaining 20 per cent typically takes place at university or is spent undertaking tasks set to meet the degree component of the apprenticeship (this is also known as off-the-job training).

There are clear differences in the way the SWDA is designed when considered against more traditional social work training routes. For example, apprentices must be employed for the entire apprenticeship period to be eligible for funding (DfE, 2024). There are also differences when it comes to regulating apprenticeships; this includes Social Work England and Ofsted, who are involved in approving and inspecting the SWDA (DfE, 2024; Ofsted, 2024). Apprenticeships are also heavily influenced and shaped by industry partners, who have a key role in the development of the curriculum and contribute to the overall delivery of the SWDA. Indeed, a core aspect of any apprenticeship is that employers lead on the development of the apprenticeship standard. If you take a look at the Institute for Apprenticeships (IfATE) website,[1] you will see a long list of employers involved in creating and updating the Social Worker (integrated degree) Apprenticeship Standard.

This chapter explores some of the key aspects unique to the apprenticeship, including the social worker (integrated degree) apprenticeship standard (often referred to as 'the standard' for ease); the Occupation Duties which are underpinned by the knowledge, skills and behaviour statements (widely known as the KSBs); and off-the-job training (perhaps better understood as academic learning, where you spend time at university); finally, this chapter will outline the End Point Assessment (EPA), which has changed considerably with the updated version of the standard, introduced in January 2023.

How has the social work apprenticeship standard developed?

It is perhaps easier to start with the role of the Trailblazer Group, as they lead the development work for all apprenticeships, which takes place prior

---

[1] The social worker (integrated degree) apprenticeship standard and assessment plan can be located here: Social Worker (integrated degree) / Institute for Apprenticeships and Technical Education

to a standard being approved by the Institute for Apprenticeships and Technical Education (IfATE). With support from IfATE, the Trailblazer Group develops a new apprenticeship standard for a particular occupation. Once an apprenticeship is approved for delivery, the Trailblazer Group remains active and will respond to any changes proposed by experts within the sector. There is typically a Trailblazer Chair who oversees the group membership, ensuring this is representative of the employers likely to use the apprenticeship (IfATE, 2023). Non-employers can also be asked to join to advise a Trailblazer Group, including representatives from training providers – including academics. Whilst non-employers can be invited to join and participate, it is the group's employers that make the final decisions on the development of the standard (IfATE, 2023).

In the case of social work, the Trailblazer Group formed some months prior to the final sign off of the initial standard, and during this development period, the group worked collaboratively to write the occupational standard (IfATE, 2023). The group also wrote the end-point assessment plan and collated information to inform the funding band allocated to social work (IfATE, 2018, 2023). This collaboration between universities (training providers) and industry partners is essential to ensure apprenticeships meet both the academic and industry practice requirements.

Towards the end of 2022, once employers and universities had developed a greater understanding of the social work apprenticeship and had overseen a full delivery of the level 6 pathway, the Trailblazer Group responded to calls for revisions to the standard. After a period of four years, the sector had learnt a lot about the delivery of the SWDA, particularly the EPA, which many felt was far too burdensome for those undertaking the SWDA route. Before any changes could be made to an apprenticeship standard, the suggested amendments were put out to consultation to gather feedback about the practicalities of any proposed changes (Turner et al., 2023). Following a consultation period and liaison with Social Work England and IfATE, the social worker apprenticeship standard was updated in January 2023. A key change introduced was around the requirements and delivery of the EPA - which, in its inception, seemed straightforward; however, in practice, this final assessment was complex for both apprentice learners and also for those of us leading the EPA activity, which will explored later on in this chapter. Further changes included: minor amendments to the KSBs; the introduction of occupation duties; and agreement for the apprenticeship standard to be delivered as part of level 7 academic provision (the apprenticeship standard itself remains a level 6 qualification). The following sections unpack some of these key changes and considers how you, the apprentice learner, can go about gathering evidence to meet the apprenticeship standard during your training.

The social work degree apprenticeship standard: occupation duties

Before moving on to explore the KSBs in greater depth, it is important to mention the introduction of the occupation duties and the recent changes to the structure of the standard. The occupation duties were first introduced when the standard was updated, this was in line with changes IfATE were introducing to ensure a greater level of consistency across apprenticeships. In essence, the occupation duties superseded the previous areas of work. During the revision of the standard, the Trailblazer Group followed the updated guidance issued by IfATE, which described a duty as 'what someone within the occupation *usually* does in the workplace' (IfATE, 2023). The guidance describes how duties should be distinct and complete activities, that they should not simply be tasks that make up part of a duty (IfATE, 2023). An example of a *complete activity* might include undertaking a comprehensive assessment of a family's needs, which would allow you to demonstrate a number of the KSBs outlined in Duty 12.

Whilst the original SWDA standard included important skills, such as 'be aware of the impact of your own values on practice' (IfATE, 2018), the introduction of occupation duties appears to have placed a greater level of accountability on apprentice learners in terms of their professional conduct. The skill, outlined above around values, is now reflected within Duty 2 of the current standard, which states:

> Be an accountable professional acting in the best interests of people that use services, by valuing each person as an individual and promoting their rights, and recognising strengths, and abilities.
>
> (IfATE, 2023)

When updating the standard, the Trailblazer Group revisited the current Professional Standards set by Social Work England to ensure a closer alignment between the professional standards (SWE, 2019) and the occupation duties (IfATE, 2023). As per IfATE's guidance, there are now a total of nineteen occupation duties outlined in the current version of the social worker apprenticeship standard (IfATE, 2023).

Reflective activity 3.1

Obtain a copy of the current social worker apprenticeship standard (IfATE, 2023) and current Social Work England Professional Standards (SWE, 2019).

Next, locate the occupation duties (apprenticeship standard) and cross reference these to the current Social Work England Professional Standards (SWE, 2019). Can you spot any similarities?

This short activity will help you to become more familiar and confident with the apprenticeship standard and also Social Work England Professional Standards, which underpin the social work profession.

The knowledge, skills and behaviour statements

The KSBs are what apprentice learners are required to demonstrate and evidence in terms of their competency in order to meet the nineteen occupation duties. The KSBs are cumulative, which means the evidence is gathered over the duration of the apprenticeship programme, and it is a requirement that each KSB is clearly evidenced and documented by the end of the course. Within my role as a university tutor, many apprentices have asked how many times they need to meet each of the KSBs. There is no simple formula for this, some universities may provide helpful ways to track KSBs – such methods are often built into ePortfolios, which are considered as part of the review meeting process. Your progress against each duty will also be closely tracked by your workplace mentor, your university tutor and practice educator (when on placement), who will help you to focus on areas where you may need more experience or knowledge.

There will be key points in the programme where you will be asked to undertake self-assessments, which often involve scoring yourself on a scale of 1–10 about how confident you feel in regard to a particular area of knowledge or skill. The first time you will be asked to undertake a self-assessment will likely be at the start of your degree, during your onboarding to the apprenticeship programme. This assessment is often referred to as an initial skills scan (DfE, 2024). It is likely that each university will have their own format or method for this initial self-assessment; some may have a tick box scaling approach, and others may request more detail and some explanation as to why you have scored yourself in a particular way. You could discuss this with your workplace mentor or line manager and make time for some reflective space, to really think about your skills and knowledge. It might be that you have been a social care worker or early help worker for several years and feel you have many transferrable skills, so you might score yourself slightly higher in some areas.

The advice I usually provide to apprentices is that, whilst you may bring key skills and experience with you, this initial self-assessment is asking you to score yourself against the KSBs for *social work*, so maybe this is something to consider further. You are about to commence training to become a social worker, and although your existing skills, knowledge and experience may provide a good foundation, it is unlikely that you will be scoring too highly at this point when you are just starting out. Naturally, as you develop your knowledge of social work theory, values, research, law, etc. and begin to apply this in your practice, we would hope to see your self-scoring against the KSBs increase as you move through the programme. In summary, the initial skills assessment helps all those involved to establish your existing abilities, it is an evaluation to determine your current skills, knowledge and understanding and to identify any areas where you may also require additional support.

It is also important to mention that if you feel you have considerable prior learning and experience that is social work specific, ensure you speak to your university tutor and employer at the very beginning when you are applying for the course, as there are clear parameters around not duplicating knowledge and skills you may already have (DfE, 2023). A lot of what happens on apprenticeships (all apprenticeships, not just social work) is guided by the apprenticeship funding rules (DfE, 2024). This is not something you need to worry about, as your employer and the university will ensure the relevant plans are in place to meet the funding rules requirements. It is, however, important that you know there are robust structures in place to ensure you have what you need and feel well supported as you embark on your social work apprenticeship.

When considering the *behaviour* component of the KSBs, apart from some very minor changes to the first statement (B1), the five behaviours approved in the original standard remain the same. The key change here is that the five behaviours are now more integrated and mapped against each of the occupation duties. The behaviours outlined in the standard are as follows:

B1: Communicate openly, honestly and accurately. Listen to people and apply professional curiosity to evaluate and assess the information needed to provide quality advice, support or care.

B2: Treat people with compassion, dignity and respect and work together to empower positive change.

B3: Adapt your approach according to the situation and context.

B4: Commit to continuous learning within social work, with curiosity and critical reflection.

B5: Adhere to the Social Work England Standards of Conduct.

(IfATE, 2023)

In relation to the knowledge and skills statements, again, apart from some very minor changes, the statements are largely the same as those identified in the original standard (IfATE, 2018). When considering what is meant by the *Knowledge* component of the KSBs, this simply means the 'information, technical detail, and "know-how" that someone needs to have and understand to carry out the duties' (IfATE, 2023). There will be many ways to evidence your learning as you move through the apprenticeship degree, and the time you spend at university is a key aspect of developing your social work knowledge. It is helpful to think about the knowledge component as the learning you need to engage with in order to carry out the work of a social worker safely and competently. When considering the *skills* component, this is referring to the practical application of knowledge needed in order to successfully undertake the occupational duties (IfATE, 2024). The skills set out in the social worker standard are learnt through on- and / or off-the-job training or experience.

The Trailblazer Group completed considerable work during the initial stages of developing the SWDA and very carefully crafted each of the KSBs. The current standard includes a helpful numbering system, so it is now much clearer to see that there is a total of thirty-five knowledge statements, fifty skills statements and five behaviour statements.

Tracking knowledge, skills and behaviours during progress reviews

The mapping of KSBs against each of the duties will be helpful when it comes to tracking your evidence during progress review meetings, direct observations, supervision and placement periods. Although there are a range of methods used to assess your progress during the SWDA, the way this is monitored and evaluated typically takes place during the progress review meetings, which currently must take place approximately every three calendar months. Any changes to the frequency of review meetings must be discussed and agreed with the employer and clearly documented within the review paperwork. The review must be a three-way discussion between you the apprentice learner, your employer and also the university (DfE, 2024). You may also have a practice educator and / or workplace mentor present depending on the model of practice in place. The progress reviews can take place face to face or virtually (for example using Microsoft Teams) or can be completed in other ways. However, given the complexities of social work, it is advisable to undertake progress reviews via meeting form wherever possible, with all parties contributing.

During progress reviews, university tutors check your progress against any actions identified at the previous review and capture any additional training you have completed – particularly that which sits outside of your off-the-job training (university learning). Checks are completed against your agreed training plan, and any gaps in learning are discussed. It is also an opportunity to explore new learning opportunities with the employer, which will enable you the apprentice learner to demonstrate practical application of the KSBs. It might be that you have a particular interest in gaining experience in attending court and developing your confidence in applying your legal knowledge or preparing a report to present at panel.

Progress reviews provide an opportunity to review your competencies and to plan for the next review period; this may also include plans for practice learning as set out by Social Work England, which stipulate all social work students spend at least 200 days (including up to thirty skills days) gaining different experiences and learning in practice settings (SWE, 2021). As outlined at the beginning of this chapter, the SWDA is approved and regulated by a number of regulatory bodies, all of which have their own set of regulatory requirements. Whilst there is often common ground, work-based learning and / or *placements* is an area that can cause some dispute, especially when considering whether on-the-job training can also be classed as placement days. This debate is beyond the scope of this chapter; however, what is absolutely clear is the requirement that all social work students (including social work apprentices) will have 'placements in at least two practice settings providing contrasting experiences . . . providing experience of sufficient numbers of statutory social work tasks involving high risk decision making and legal interventions' (SWE, 2021).

The review process also allows for any concerns or changes in circumstances to be discussed, including a change in line manager or workplace mentor or additional information relevant to learning difficulties and disability concerns or learning support needs (DfE, 2024). There are often frequent changes regarding the requirements and timings of progress reviews; those outlined here are reflective of the most recent changes set out in the funding rules dated August 2024 (DfE, 2024).

Top tips

How to prepare for a progress review

- You will need to ensure your ePortfolio reflects an up-to-date record of your off-the-job learning hours.
- Complete a self-assessment against the KSBs to determine areas of progress since the last review, and have examples to hand in for discussion during the review.
- Make sure you have met with your line manager and / or workplace mentor to discuss key aspects of your work so that this can be captured in the review report.
- Be prepared to talk about any direct observations that have taken place, and share any key reflections from supervision sessions and / or placement / work-based learning.

How do I evidence the knowledge, skills and behaviours?

Whilst you can provide specific examples against each KSB, such as demonstrating your communication (B1) or treating someone with compassion and respect (B2), it is perhaps more helpful to consider the

KSBs from a holistic perspective, as several are likely to interconnect during any given piece of work. The following case examples illustrate how you can capture evidence against the occupation duties and KSBs.

Case example 1

Let's imagine you are approaching a progress review (these must take place at least every 3 calendar months); this is your second review meeting in year two of the SWDA (DfE, 2024). The review is a progress discussion, including you the apprentice learner, the university tutor, employer and workplace mentor. During the progress review, checks are completed against any actions agreed at the previous review meeting, including any training you may have completed. The review also allows for any off-the-job training evidence, including any new learning that takes place outside of what you learn at university; this may include new knowledge developed in the workplace.

Ahead of the review meeting, you have had regular supervision sessions with your workplace mentor; you have successfully completed a direct observation and have passed two university modules. In preparation for the progress meeting, you will complete a report outlining the key evidence gathered from the current review period. You should also include a self-assessment score and outline any areas of development for over the next review period. The table below provides a sample of how you might approach this activity.

Summary of evidence towards the achievement of standards and requirements that have been demonstrated over the review period	
Duty 1 Promote the rights, strengths and well-being of people, families and communities to ensure their voice and expertise is heard and acknowledged. **KSBs** K1 K3 K5 K6 K7 K8 K9 K13 K20 K22 K23 K24 K27 K28 S3 S5 S6 S7 S8 S41 B2 B5	**Self-assessment** K3 - 8/10 K20 - 7/10 K22 - 7/10 S3 - 7/10 S5 - 8/10 S6 - 8/10 B2 - 9/10

Update from apprentice:
As a result of completing my 70-day placement in an adult social care team, my knowledge and understanding of the Care Act 2014 has developed considerably. During placement, I supported social workers to respond to referrals received from other professionals regarding vulnerable adults. My practice educator supported me to understand the importance of responding to safeguarding concerns.

Whilst I had learnt about s.42 of the Care Act 2014 in the recent safeguarding module, it really helped to see how to apply this knowledge in practice. In supervision, we discussed the six safeguarding principles and the eligibility criteria for service provision (K20, K22).

Update from workplace mentor / practice educator:
To date, the apprentice has demonstrated a good awareness of the key stages of a s.42 safeguarding inquiry. They have had an opportunity to apply their knowledge of Making Safeguarding Personal and the importance of involving the adult at risk or their representative. I have been impressed with their level of knowledge around the different forms of abuse and neglect and recognizing the signs of harm (K20, K22).

A consistent strength in the apprentice's practice is identifying an individual's rights and advocating for their rights to be promoted or upheld (S5). They support individuals to share their views by developing professional and respectful relationships and completing person centred assessments (K3; B2; B5).

The apprentice's practice experience, combined with developing a deeper understanding of legislation and awareness of the impact of their own values, has refined their assessment skills (S3). They have evidenced their ability to extract information, identify needs and eligibility, assess risk, critically analyse information, triangulate information from other sources, complete support plans, assess capacity and facilitate best interest decisions.

Each progress report will capture some degree of evidence against a number of the apprenticeship duties; as stated earlier, KSBs are cumulative, which means apprentices are expected to build on their KSBs progressively throughout the apprenticeship.

Case example 2

This time lets imagine you are near the end of your final 100-day placement, which you have completed within the organization where you are employed. This has been a contrasting experience; you are usually based within the children and families' team but have joined the 16+ team to gain a broader understanding of different systems in operation. You are now near the end of the SWDA, and your confidence and depth of knowledge has progressed, which should be reflected in your self-assessment. We should not typically see apprentice leaners scoring themselves 9/10 and 10/10 on their self-assessments until they head towards the end of their studies and have developed the required KSBs. Your journey on the SWDA should be incremental and there should be space for stretch and challenge across each level of the programme.

Summary of evidence towards the achievement of standards and requirements that have been demonstrated over the review period

Duty 6 Work directly with individuals and their families through the professional use of self, using interpersonal skills to develop relationships based on openness and transparency.	**Self-assessment**

Duty 6 Work directly with individuals and their families through the professional use of self, using interpersonal skills to develop relationships based on openness and transparency.

Self-assessment

K4 - 9/10
K8 - 9/10
K12 - 8/10
K22 - 9/10
S5 - 9/10
S10 - 9/10
S11- 9/10
S27 - 10/10
S40 - 9/10
B1 - 9/10
B5 - 9/10

KSBs
K3 K4 K7 K8 K9 K11 K12 K22 K23 K24 K25 K26 K27 K28
S5 S7 S12 S13 S19 S34 S35 S38 S39
B1 B2 B3 B5

Duty 13 Work with relevant colleagues and agencies to support people experiencing difficult situations, to gather information and to make timely decisions when positive change is not evident.

KSBs
K4 K15 K16 K17 K18 K22 K23 K24 K28 K29 K30
S8 S11 S12 S13 S27 S40 S41
B1 B5

Update from apprentice:
During my final 100-day placement, I was based in the 16+ team, where I supported young people leaving local authority care and moving into independence. I was responsible for completing Pathway Plans and offering support to young people until the age of 25 (S8, S39). I found this contrasting experience to be invaluable and felt I learnt a lot about enabling and empowering young people rather than taking on their tasks and responsibilities. I have been supporting a group of young people who have experienced trauma during their childhood, which has had an impact on their emotional well-being and mental health (K14). Due to the ages of the young people, I have applied a wide range of legislation including the Children (Leaving Care) Act 2000, Children Act 1989, Care Act 2014 and the Children and Social Work Act 2017 (S42, S45).

Update from workplace mentor / practice educator:
Since the last review meeting, the apprentice has developed their confidence, especially when applying key legislation, which was an area identified at the last progress meeting (K20). They have demonstrated their ability to develop positive relationships with young people and have embedded the Signs of Safety approach consistently in their work (K12). I have been particularly impressed with their recording and report writing skills; case records are completed to a high standard (S42).

During the past few weeks, the apprentice has taken a lead on completing an assessment which has involved reading referrals, gathering information, weighing up risks and protective factors and determining the level of support and intervention required (S43, S45). During supervision, we used a range of reflective models to aid our thinking, and the apprentice has really considered what might be going on for a particular young person and the reasons why they are behaving in a certain way (S30, S44). The apprentice has an excellent working understanding of child exploitation, which informed their thinking when supporting young people (K10, K14).

Off-the-job training

Whilst different training providers may employ a range of delivery models, a typical delivery model involves apprentices spending one day a week at university. This day at university is officially known as off-the-job training, which is training received during your practical period and during your normal working hours for the purpose of achieving the KSBs outlined in the SWDA (DfE, 2023). You may also hear the term 'on-the-job training', which you receive from your employer for the sole purpose of enabling you to perform the work for which you are employed.

Before we move on, it is important to first outline off-the-job training in more detail, so that you are confident about what this means. Off-the-job training is defined as learning that is undertaken outside of day-to-day work duties and leads towards achieving the apprenticeship (IfATE, 2023). If you are a full-time apprentice (working at least thirty hours per week), you should receive a minimum of six hours of off-the-job training (this equates to the minimum requirement of 20 per cent new learning). Although you will be at university and / or undertaking work set by the university during these six hours, this is still work time, as your organization is releasing you to undertake this training. This means your attendance is a requirement, and you should inform your line manager if you are not able to attend your off-the-job training day.

An apprenticeship is a work-based programme, and it is therefore reasonable that the 20 per cent off-the-job training is delivered during your typical working hours. It would be unfair to expect you to complete this new learning after your contracted hours or at weekends. The specific day per week allocated to off-the-job training is negotiated between the university and the employer and should consider the needs of all involved. As outlined by the DfE (2023), off-the-job training is a statutory requirement for an English apprenticeship. The university must verify that the off-the-job training delivered to the apprentice meets the following definition:

> It is training which is received by the apprentice within their practical period, during the apprentice's normal working hours, for the purpose of achieving the knowledge, skills and behaviours of the apprenticeship they are undertaking. By normal working hours we mean the hours for which the apprentice would normally be paid, excluding overtime.
>
> (DfE, 2023:5)

All apprentices are required to record their off-the-job training time, including the number of hours and the activities undertaken. The university will likely have some form of ePortfolio system which will allow you to track and record the off-the-job hours you complete. This ePortfolio is where you will also complete reflective logs which capture key learning from your off-the-job training. A key aspect of your off-the-job training is that it must be relevant to the apprenticeship (IfATE, 2023); this means the knowledge you develop during your off-the-job training must align to the social worker apprenticeship standard.

What can be included as off-the-job training?

The apprenticeship funding rules set out clear parameters about what can be included as off-the-job training, and the activities set are often directed by the university (DfE, 2023). Depending on the model of delivery (each university will deliver their programmes slightly differently), you will participate in teaching sessions, which may include both individual and group learning; attending and contributing during lectures; simulation activities; seminars; and tutorials. The apprenticeship funding rules (DfE, 2023) state the following activities can be included in off-the-job training:

- The teaching of theory (e.g. lectures, role-playing, simulation exercises and online learning).
- Practical training (e.g. shadowing, mentoring, industry visits).
- Learning support.
- Time spent writing assignments and projects.
- Revision (where this is specifically required for achievement of the apprenticeship).

Whilst a large proportion of off-the-job training is often delivered via classroom-based activity, particularly in social work, there is some flexibility, and off-the-job training can also take place at apprentices' usual place of work or at an external location. What is important to remember here is that for an activity to be included as off-the-job, it must teach *new* knowledge, skills and behaviours and be directly relevant to the apprenticeship standard (DfE, 2023).

In recent years, there has been a gradual increase in online learning; however, this was accelerated by the Covid-19 pandemic, which resulted in most programmes moving to online teaching (Simanovic et al., 2021). This shift had particular challenges for practice-based degrees such as social work, which is a relational discipline and prepares students and apprentices for working directly (and in person) with children, families and communities (Smoyer et al., 2020). That said, many providers have developed a range of delivery styles to suit current employer and apprentice needs, so you may experience a very different delivery of the SWDA compared to colleagues completing the programme at a neighbouring university. It is important to keep track of your off-the-job training and share this at your progress reviews. In preparation, you may want to note down the date and time of the session; name of the training provider or organization; a description of the topics or skills covered; and any assessments or tasks completed. Below is an example of how you might record off-the-job training / activities.

Off-the-job training record example
20/01/2025 – 11/04/2025

Date	Day	Activity	Description	Hours	Evidence recorded on portfolio
20/01/2025	Monday 9.30–16.30	Lecture	Module 1 session 1 Professional standards	6	Yes – register and group task
28/01/2025	Tuesday 9.30–16.30	Training	Safeguarding Adults Training	6	Yes – cert. of attendance
10/02/2025	Monday 9.30–16.30	Lecture	Module 1 session 4 Relationship-based practice	6	Yes – register
19/02/2025	Wednesday 10.00–18.00	Shadowing	Day with the child protection team	6	Yes – reflective log
10/03/2025	Monday 9.00–16.00	Simulation	Module 2 session 2 Social work theory	6	Yes – register and article summary
04/04/2025	Friday 10.00–17.00	Training	Mental health and well-being training	6	Yes – cert. of attendance and discussed in supervision

Many universities will ask apprentice learners to complete reflective logs or learning journals as part of their ePortfolio as a way of capturing their thoughts, reflections and insights from each training session. This is an effective way of evidencing your personal growth beyond attendance and module assessments and enables you to identify your own learning goals and areas of development. I particularly like the model where apprentice learners complete a short reflective log based on their off-the-job training and then share this log with their workplace mentor ahead of supervision, and together they review the learning and consider any progress against the KSBs.

Top tips

Recording off-the-job training

- Keep a detailed calendar of your off-the-job training – record dates, times and location of each training session you attend or activity you complete.
- Capture key information about each activity, including a description of the topics and skills covered; try and make links to your KSBs. Ensure your new learning is well evidenced.
- Write a short reflective log capturing your thoughts and reflections; share this with your workplace mentor and discuss your learning during supervision.

The importance of stretch and challenge during the apprenticeship

Some apprentice learners embarking on the SWDA might think they are *doing social work already*. If you are amongst those who believe this, please take a few moments to reflect on this further and consider the potential implications of this starting position. Perhaps consider your current knowledge of statutory responsibilities and regulatory requirements, your application of the legal frameworks and the importance of evidence-informed practice. Are you familiar with Social Work England's professional standards? Suggesting that you are *doing social work already* is rather shortsighted and indicates a limited awareness of what social work entails, both professionally and academically (Stone and Shannon, 2022). Whilst many apprentices might have several years' experience in social care settings and have undertaken tasks that have much in common with those undertaken by social workers, apprentices have not yet developed the requisite KSBs to do social work. It is important for apprentice learners to appreciate this.

If you are applying to join the SWDA, it is important to recognize that for most (aside of any recognition of prior learning), this is the start of your social work learning journey. During the initial months of the SWDA, you will largely continue with the work for which you have been employed; apart from your off-the-job day, your week will likely look the same. At this stage, you are encouraged to be consciously aware of the KSBs you are developing and how you might apply or practise these new skills. You will be looking to apply new learning so that this becomes embedded in your work (DfE, 2023). As you progress through the apprenticeship, you will continue to demonstrate your progress via direct observations, supervision, academic work and progress reviews. These various forms of assessment take place both in the workplace and university setting, and a range of people will be involved and contribute to the assessment of apprentices. The academic team at your allocated training provider has a key role in assessing the degree component of the SWDA, ensuring that apprentice learners complete all summative assessments (these typically happen at the end of a module or placement period). Line managers, workplace mentors and practice educators take the lead in assessing the workplace component and ensuring apprentices have access to a diverse range of work-based learning and placement opportunities.

With support from your employer, you will identify a range of distinct and complete activities that will stretch and challenge your thinking and support your progress against the KSBs (IfATE, 2023). This might include assessment writing, attending court or delivering specific interventions or pieces of direct work. As you move through the different levels of the SWDA, you will hopefully experience increased confidence in your newly acquired KSBs and should gradually start to work more autonomously (with support and guidance). As you complete the final placement period and head towards the final stages of the course, you should have a clear overview of the evidence gathered against the occupation duties and KSBs, which will be appraised during the gateway review (there will be more on this later on). Below is an illustrative example of a supportive approach to facilitating appropriate stretch and challenge during the SWDA.

Stretch and Challenge Case Example

For the purpose of this example, lets imagine you are usually based in an adult social care team and work alongside social workers who have a duty to complete a needs assessment to determine whether a person is eligible for services. You are familiar with the key aspects of the Care Act (2014) and have contributed to several assessments within your role as a social care worker.

You have recently commenced your 100-day placement period, and your employer has arranged for you to join the Children and Family assessment team where you will be required to work with social workers who are undertaking child and family assessments. Your practice educator has reassured you about the high standard of your work and how your assessment skills are transferrable. As a social care worker, you are fairly confident when it comes to understanding the legislation underpinning adult social care, but you are feeling a little nervous about the children's legislation, especially the Children Act 1989 and the parameters of Children in Need (s.17).

In order to support you in developing new KSBs and building your confidence in completing assessments, your practice educator suggests the following approach to the work-based mentor who will be assigning work to you during the placement period.

Shadow an assessment	Co-work an assessment	Lead an assessment
During the first three weeks as part of your induction, you have several opportunities to shadow experienced social workers as they visit families, gather information, liaise with other professionals and write assessments. As part of the assessment, social workers speak directly to children and young people. This is something you are particularly nervous about, as this is a new skill to you – as you have never worked with children before.	You are now in week six and you are feeling more confident about the expectations. You have been assisting social workers in recent weeks and helping to gather relevant information and have started to undertake direct work with children. You are assigned to co-work an assessment. This means you will be helping to write each section, and you will be expected to share your analysis with the allocated social worker.	As you move further into the placement period, you are now clear on the processes; you are using your transferrable skills and are feeling more at ease communicating with children. You are assigned an assessment to lead; the social worker will be co-assigned and will oversee your work. You will arrange to see the family, talk to children, contact other professionals and gather key information. You will write the analysis and once signed off by the manager; you will share the assessment with the family and explain the next steps. The social worker will be present when you share the report.

What is the End Point Assessment?

As outlined at the beginning of this chapter, the social worker apprenticeship standard was updated in January 2023, introducing significant changes to the End Point Assessment. The original EPA had a high assessment workload for apprentices and a heavy administrative burden placed on providers and employers. As the sector developed experience in delivering the EPA, it became clear that change was needed. The EPA was reviewed and amended in line with other apprenticeship standards where a regulatory body oversees professional registration. The EPA can only commence once an apprentice learner has completed their practical period and all their off-the-job training is completed and evidenced; this is when the apprentice learner is ready to move through the gateway process and enter the end-point assessment period (DfE, 2023).

Before the EPA can begin, apprentices need to attend a Gateway Review meeting, during which a final check is completed to ensure the apprentice has met all the KSBs, passed all the required modules and completed 200 days in supervised practice / placement (IfATE, 2023). The EPA period can then commence and typically takes place within one month. As outlined in the EPA plan, the apprentice is not required to carry out any additional assessments, as the EPA is stated to be the process where: 'consideration by the examination board and notice of grade decision to Social Work England' is carried out by the training provider (IfATE, 2023: 3). Once the examination board has verified the final pass / fail decision, a pass list is sent to Social Work England advising of all the apprentices who have received a final grade that meets regulatory requirements. The key takeaway here is that the EPA is no longer credit-bearing, and there are no additional formal assessments; the EPA is simply the final examination board, and your training provider will facilitate this final action.

Chapter summary

This chapter has provided an overview of some the key aspects of the SWDA, including how the apprenticeship standard was originally developed, the recent changes to the EPA and the important role of the Trailblazer Group. The chapter has also considered and explored the KSBs and the introduction of the nineteen occupation duties. As outlined in the case examples, the

KSBs are tracked throughout the programme and reviewed at each progress meeting. It is important to remember that the KSBs are evidenced both in the workplace and university, and there are many ways apprentices can evidence their progress, including direct observations, supervision, placement periods and off-the-job training. Remember to follow my 'top tips' in preparation for progress reviews, including updating your ePortfolio! Finally, the chapter has provided a brief outline of the current EPA and the introduction of a less complex and labour-intensive process. These changes have been welcomed nationally, and it is a very positive change for all those apprentices commencing on the SWDA post 2023.

Recommended reading

Institute for Apprenticeships and Technical Education. (2023). *Social worker* (integrated degree). https://www.instituteforapprenticeships.org/apprenticeship-standards/social-worker-integrated-degree-v1-1 (accessed 15 August 2024).

Stone, C., & Shannon, M. (2022). *The social work degree apprenticeship.* Critical Publishing.

References

British Association Social Work (BASW). (2018). *Professional capability framework.* https://basw.co.uk/training-cpd/professional-capabilities-framework-pcf (accessed 15 August 2024).

Department for Education. (2023). *Apprenticeship off-the-job training version 5.* https://assets.publishing.service.gov.uk/media/6530efdb92895c000ddcba2b/2023_10_OTJT_Guide_v5_-_23_24_Rules_v1.0.pdf (accessed 26 August 2024).

Department for Education. (2023). *Guidance apprenticeships: Initial assessment to recognise prior learning.* https://www.gov.uk/government/publications/apprenticeships-recognition-of-prior-learning/apprenticeships-initial-assessment-to-recognise-prior-learning (accessed 16 August 2024).

Department for Education. (2023). *Off-the-job training myth vs fact.* https://assets.publishing.service.gov.uk/media/6530f11ad0666200131b7d16/2023_10_OTJT_Myths_-_23_24_Rules_v1.0.pdf (accessed 29 December 2024).

Department for Education. (2024). *Apprenticeship training provider accountability framework and specification*. https://www.gov.uk/government/publications/apprenticeship-training-provider-accountability-framework/apprenticeship-training-provider-accountability-framework-and-specification--2 (accessed 15 December 24).

Department for Education. (2024). *Apprenticeship funding rules version 4*. https://assets.publishing.service.gov.uk/media/666c2c5dfed5bd09e5195a58/Apprenticeship_funding_rules_2324_V4.pdf (accessed 14 December 2024).

Institute for Apprenticeships and Technical Education. (2018). *Social worker* (integrated degree). https://www.instituteforapprenticeships.org/apprenticeship-standards/social-worker-integrated-degree-v1-0 (accessed 15 August 2024).

Institute for Apprenticeships and Technical Education. (2023). *Social worker* (integrated degree). https://www.instituteforapprenticeships.org/apprenticeship-standards/social-worker-integrated-degree-v1-1 (accessed 15 August 2024).

Institute for Apprenticeships and Technical Education. (2023). *End-point assessment plan for social worker statutory integrated degree apprenticeship*. https://www.instituteforapprenticeships.org/media/6337/st0510_-social-worker-statutory-integrated-epa-_level-6_ap-for-publication_26082022.pdf (accessed 30 December 2024).

Institute for Apprenticeships and Technical Education. (2023). *Trailblazer groups*. https://www.instituteforapprenticeships.org/developing-new-apprenticeships/trailblazer-group/ (accessed 14 August 2024).

Institute for Apprenticeships and Technical Education. (2023). *Developing an occupation proposal*. https://www.instituteforapprenticeships.org/developing-new-apprenticeships/developing-an-apprenticeship-occupation-proposal/ (accessed 15 August 2024).

Institute for Apprenticeships and Technical Education. (2024). *Developing an occupational standard*. https://www.instituteforapprenticeships.org/developing-new-apprenticeships/developing-occupational-standards/ (accessed 15 August 2024).

Office for Standards in Education (Ofsted). *Education inspection framework*. https://www.gov.uk/government/publications/education-inspection-framework/education-inspection-framework-for-september-2023 (accessed 15 December 2024).

Simanovic, T. Cioarţă, I., Jardine, C., & Paul, S. (2021). Social work education during COVID-19: Students' perceptions of the challenges and opportunities of online and blended learning. *Intersectionalities, 9,* 131–41.

Smoyer, A. B., O'Brien, K., & Rodriguez-Keyes, E. (2020). Lessons learned from COVID-19: Being known in online social work classrooms. *International Social Work*, *63*, 651–4.

Social Work England. (2019) Professional standards. https://www .socialworkengland.org.uk/media/1640/1227_socialworkengland_standards _prof_standards_final-aw.pdf

Social Work England. (2021). *Education and training standards*. https://www .socialworkengland.org.uk/standards/education-and-training-standards/ (accessed 28 December 24).

Stone, C., & Shannon, M. (2022). *The social work degree apprenticeship*. Critical Publishing.

Turner, D., & Low, K. (2023). 'A significant positive impact': Delivering the end point assessment for the social work degree apprenticeship. *Social Work Education*, 1–17. https://doi.org/10.1080/02615479.2023.2187369.

Applying knowledge and theory to practice

Jordan Savage and Laura James

Chapter Outline

Why so many theories . . .?   60

The social work apprentice perspective: developing an
   understanding of the role of knowledge and theory in practice   63

Applying knowledge and theory to practice: a practice example   64

The fusing of learning as an apprentice learner   67

Framing your thinking   69

Applying theory of the 'use of self'   72

Chapter summary   76

This chapter will support you to develop your confidence in applying knowledge and theory to practice. As noted in the introductory chapter, it is quite common for social work learners to view theory and practice as two quite distinct things. Social work is an evidence-based and research-informed profession, and the more confident a social worker feels in both understanding and applying a relevant knowledge base encompassing theory, the more successful interventions in practice will be. It is crucial that as a social work apprentice you develop this key skill, as having the confidence and understanding the value of applying knowledge and theory to practice will enable you to evidence the judgements and decisions that you make.

This chapter seeks to examine a range of prevalent knowledge areas and theoretical notions in context, and in doing so, there will be examples, exercises and top tips to support you as apprentice learners to extend your thinking and develop the confidence you need to apply your new knowledge in the workplace. This chapter is particularly unique in that the main author is a former social work apprentice, who is now an experienced social worker. As a result, the content draws upon his experiences as an apprentice social worker, and the chapter examines real examples of how knowledge and theory has been applied in the workplace.

Why so many theories . . .?

When presented with the question, 'What is a theory?', some may simply say that a theory is someone's idea about something. A theory is thought to be an explanation for something – for example, why someone may present a particular behaviour or respond in a certain way or a reason for why something might happen. There are different perceptions about theory according to Thomas (2017), who seeks to explain what theory means from different discipline perspectives. Given that social work sits within applied social sciences, Thomas (2017) perceives that theory relates to the 'thinking side' of practice and views theory as an explanation that emerges from professional practice. More often than not, theories are developed on the back on a lot of research, and the theories we often think of when we think about social work are often a collection of different pioneers' ideas.

To provide some further context, attachment theory is a theory that is perceived slightly differently by a number of pioneers – Bowlby and Ainsworth, to name a couple. The theories on attachment have developed and evolved over time; they have been critiqued and also criticized yet remain a largely relevant theory within social work. Whilst there are many theories that seek to explain a person's experience or provide a rationale for why people respond in certain ways, there are also theories used within social work that can be viewed as methods or approaches to practice. Examples include strengths-based practice, task-centred practice and relationship-based practice. Each of these approaches relate to how you as an apprentice and future social worker work with those with lived experience, and so these type of theories seek to guide you in the work you undertake, how you communicate and how you build effective relationships. In the same way as the attachment theory, there are different perspectives on each of these approaches.

As you begin on your social work learning journey, the realization of the fact that there are so many different theories may at first be quite daunting. You may also find that so many of the theories you are presented with during your studies either argue, contradict or are in fact largely similar to one another. Theories support us to consider the reality of a situation, and as it is important to consider different perspectives in social work practice, it is more often helpful than not to have a range of theoretical perspectives to draw upon (Howe & Hill, 2024).

As you begin to apply theory to practice, you may find yourself thinking: which theory should I choose? How will I know if it's the right one? Are there others that may suit the situation better? These questions can pose a further challenge as, quite often, when you engage in reading around theory, you will often be presented with different viewpoints for the same theory, and different authors may seek to celebrate the strengths of one theory, whereas others may look to critique the limitations of the said theory. There is usually always a bias in theoretical viewpoints, and this is why it is helpful to explore different perspectives in order to consider which theory would be best suited to the situation you intend to apply it to. Considering different perspectives will also support you to develop your critical thinking skills (which will be covered in detail in Chapter 8).

Whilst you may begin your apprenticeship with the daunting thought of having to learn about a range of theories, it is important to think about what you may already know, as the chances are you already have some prior knowledge that you build upon. Whilst you may not necessarily know the names of a lot of the theories at the beginning of your journey, you will likely know that there are reasons why things are done a certain way in practice, and you will likely know that through assessing the needs of those with lived experience, there is often some kind of knowledge drawn upon that supports you to understand the experiences of those you are working with.

Reflective thoughts

Irrespective of where you are on your apprenticeship learning journey, consider how many social work-related theories you are aware of at this point in your learning journey. How many of these are similar to one another?

How many contradict one another?

Which ones do you think would help you when undertaking an assessment of need for a person with lived experience?

Which ones seek to explain why something has happened / how someone has responded?

Which ones do you think apply to how you as an apprentice communicate with those you work with?

Reflective activity 4.1

Have a think about the following three theories that are relevant to social work:

- Attachment theory.
- Grief and loss.
- Empowerment theory.

See if you can find three different sources that talk about these theories. Think about the following:

- What are the different perspectives presented by each author?
- Can you identify the strengths and limitations of each theory?
- Could you apply one of these theories to a piece of work you are undertaking in the workplace?
- If you feel you are not yet confident in being able to apply the theories to practice, what else do you need to know? How can you achieve this?

Some resources you might find useful when undertaking this activity:

- YouTube has lots of videos that explain social work theory well. Siobhan Maclean has a number of videos of YouTube that usually demystify social work theory – her videos may be a great starting point which will give you confidence in seeking out further sources / literature.

- Your university library: there will likely be lots of online databases you can access with your university login details.
- Physical books on social work theory, such as Howe and Hill (2024).

The social work apprentice perspective: developing an understanding of the role of knowledge and theory in practice

As an apprentice that was working with families and young people, it was striking how time spent in lecture theatres and seminars allowed for contextualizing module learning directly into practice. This notion developed a parallel way of learning and thinking. On the one hand, you are present in the moment as a learner – concerned for the module assignment task at hand, absorbing the knowledge and theory being presented and considering how this may be structured in an essay – to ensure you project an understanding to meet the required learning objectives and achieve the required pass.

On the other hand, there is the unique benefit of being an apprentice social worker at play. Whilst the theory, knowledge, skills and approaches are being absorbed, you have the parallel thought of your working life becoming apparent in your thoughts. The theories begin to wrap around the lived experiences of the people that you work with. The social histories and the interactions between yourself and the person with lived experience begin to fit with the notions that are being discussed. Ideas are inspired as to how best approach the next direct work session, how to better convey an understanding and how you may better empower those you work with in the coming weeks. Cases long past also enter your thoughts and develop new meaning because of the new knowledge you have gained. Reimagined past work experience evolves into a foundation to be built upon in relation to how things may be approached differently should similar scenarios be encountered in the future.

As these two parallel trains of thought fuse, they mutually benefit each other in terms of portraying a better understanding within the context of presenting theory and knowledge within an essay and, additionally, in improving practice. I found more and more that I was not only note taking in terms of my academic student life but adding notes in margins relating to events and circumstances in relation to the people with lived experience whom I was working with and how the theory and knowledge could benefit my practice to support the families and young people I was working with whilst being an apprentice social worker. Developing this process beyond thought over the course of the apprenticeship and making it part of my active reflection further developed a growing purposeful use of theory and knowledge within the casework I was undertaking away from the university, which was complimented by making use of the access to university libraries.

This has been an invaluable learning experience for me where I feel my level of critical thinking has significantly developed. As I am now qualified as a social worker and work in a multi-agency safeguarding team, I have a broad knowledge of theory relevant to working with families and have understood the relevance and importance of research-informed practice, especially in a fast-paced role. Overall, having the opportunity to apply knowledge and theory in my daily practice has been essential to my learning, in addition to developing an in depth knowledge of legislation and relevant thresholds, which I have also been able to apply within the workplace to really solidify my knowledgebase.

Furthermore, regarding the day-to-day work, this has enabled me to progress to a research practitioner role, where those early thought processes have developed into not only applying knowledge but, now, additionally trying to create knowledge through research projects.

Applying knowledge and theory to practice: a practice example

Whilst working as a family support worker (prior to becoming a social work apprentice), it was important that I had the right knowledge base and a basic understanding of theory, as this knowledge base underpinned the work I was undertaking, for example, one to one direct work sessions; however, the explicit reference to the knowledge base and theory was not exactly present nor required. For example, a knowledge of attachment theory and child development was key; however, it was equally as important to draw upon the assessment framework in observations that would be acknowledged and fed back to the social worker, who would then utilize in their assessment.

To return to the earlier point, whereby learning through attendance to lectures and seminars was acknowledged, this step from working in a family support role as an apprentice social worker is perhaps symbolic of how the development goes beyond the observable and becomes evidence-based practice. This can be noted in an example writing about a family time session between a mother and her child (please note the example is fictious), whereby observations made within the family time session were framed in a way that evidenced the importance of the application of knowledge and theory.

Practice example

Within the first five minutes of the observation, it was noted that Leonard made some gestures and large movements above age related expectations: climbing upon the chair, sitting crossed leg-ged and also bouncing to jump off (Sheridan et al., 1997). Emotional warmth, as noted within HM Government (2018), was also noted between Leonard and his mum in the form of hugs during the first ten minutes whilst choosing which DVD to watch on the TV. These factors drawing upon attachment and the interactions between parent and child were necessary for the co-construction of internal working models as proposed by Bowlby (1988) and further developed by Bretherton (1993). In this instance in particular, Fahlberg's (1991) positive interaction cycle was necessary for building self-worth and emotional regulation through hugs and, thus, supporting emotional and behavioural development.

The above is a very brief snippet of what was a lovely start to a family time session but something that is observable in everyday life. The notions drawn from the theories selected are things that you, as practitioners prior to becoming apprentice social workers, may already be familiar with; however, quite often, once you begin to engage in social work learning, your understanding is solidified, and the application to practice becomes much easier and much more meaningful too. It can often be the case that prior to engaging in social work learning, you may have an awareness of a range of theories but do not necessarily know how to apply them, or indeed, you may not feel confident in your own comprehension of the theories; this is very normal.

Let's now think about the practice example given above in a little more detail in order to further examine the application in detail.

Sheridan et al. (1997) writes about early development and frames this in terms of age-related expectations, in which practitioners working with children, young people and families may often refer to. As an apprentice social worker, you will likely learn about different theoretical perspectives on child development, as these form a part of assessment and identification of need, and so the example explored both above and below should give you a sense of how to apply one of the well-known theories. Attachments are key to how we view interactions within family dynamics and are acknowledged within the example. Attachment theory is likely to be one of the first theories you are introduced to on your social worker learning journey and probably one of the main theories that you will keep coming back to, as attachment theory can be applied across the life course and there is so much literature on the theory. Finally, the example above makes reference to the assessment framework within an HM Government (2018) document when acknowledging emotional warmth. This framework is evidence-based and theory informed, and across both the adult and child workforce, there are different frameworks which are used as a basis to inform assessment and decision-making.

Whilst you may be familiar with some of the concepts identified above, or indeed you may not be, the importance of demonstrating awareness of relevant knowledge and theory and ultimately being able to use knowledge and theory to identify and evidence a person's strengths and needs is key. In being able to do this, you will be able to consider how the needs you have identified can be supported; action planning and targeted intervention would then follow. Below is a further practice example that follows on from the one above.

Practice example

Leonard presented some moments of speech which appeared to be guided by his mother. This, however, appeared to suggest that Leonard's speech was possibly at a level below his chronological age. Sheridan et al. (1997) would assert that Leonard, aged three years, should be asking questions continually and using signifi-cant amounts of recognisable words. Observations suggest that Leonard's speech sits more comfortably within the age of eighteen months, as his speech was more echoed in short sentences, joining in with nursery rhymes. Leonard's speech appeared to be linked to certain tasks, such as 'tidy up time', 'coat on' and 'shoes on', which he mimicked back whilst altering behaviour towards the task associated. Within the realms of behaviourism, it could be argued that this is an example of conditioning, where associations have been rein-forced and strengthened (Watson & Rayner, 1920).

The observation above highlights how drawing upon relevant theory and knowledge has identified that there may be a delay in the child's speech and language and, therefore, allows the practitioner to consider whether a referral to health services, such as the speech and language team, would be useful. The application of theory and knowledge will also support the practitioner to consider what support the mother may need to support the child's development.

Top tip

- Think about the recent practice examples shared, and explore what resources and tools are available to you in order to develop your confidence further. Supervision is a useful tool, and often, your workplace mentor and your Practice Educator, when on placement, will have different resources to support you to develop your application skills further.

The fusing of learning as an apprentice learner

To think back to the earlier concept that was introduced in relation to the fusing of learning in the lecture theatre into practical working life, it is worth introducing an additional concept to further support you to think about the value of applying your learning to practice. Einstein once said that 'imagination is more important than knowledge'; there is a belief that this is applicable to how we apply knowledge to practice. Empathic imagination is perhaps the necessary glue that fuses earlier descriptions of taking the lecture theatre learning and considering how this translates to the work you do with those with lived experience. It is how we empathically imagine the lives of those we work with through their social histories and our experiences with them that allows our mind's eye to connect and link with the relevant theory, use this to the benefit of empowering others and better develop our practice in learning what works, what the best fit is and what might not be the best theory (Buckner, 2010; Schacter et al., 2008). As a result, one of the added benefits of being a social work apprentice learner is that you will have an abundance of opportunities to directly explore and apply the material from your academic learning within current and real life settings with real people.

Reflective activity 4.2

Think about a piece of work / intervention you are undertaking with a person with lived experience in the workplace.

Utilizing Rolfe et al's (2001) reflective framework, try to answer the following questions:

What?

Describe five minutes from an interaction you have had or an observation you have undertaken. What was apparent in relation to the person's presentation, behaviour, environment?

So what?

What theory would support you to understand / unpack the interaction or observation further? What could the person's presentation, behaviour or environment indicate? Was there something that stood out to you? What does relevant literature say about the theory you have chosen, and can you make a connection from it to the person you are working with? Are other theories relevant? Is there a framework you can draw upon, or is there a piece of specialist knowledge you would benefit from knowing about in order to better your understanding of the person's lived experience?

Now what?

Now that you have used theory to analyse the interaction or observation, what actions do you now have? Have you identified some support needs? Is a referral to another service needed? Is there more information you need to seek to support the professional judgements you will make about the needs of this person? Do you need to do something else?

Framing your thinking

Whilst the practice example above relates mostly to children's social work, the concepts explored are the same irrespective of which part of the sector you currently work in. The idea of considering which areas of knowledge or which theory may be appropriate to apply in practice can feel very daunting as a new learner (or even as a learner further on in your studies). In order to be in a position to begin to think about which theory, for example, you may choose to apply, it is crucial that you first spend time getting to know the person you are working with, understand their history, read any previous case notes and speak to others who may have information. In doing this, you are able to paint a metaphorical picture, and in doing so, you will be surprised at how many theories or concepts discussed in the classroom setting come to mind.

The following 'past, present and future framework' may support you to think about how you can apply the relevant theory and knowledge to the direct work you undertake with those who have lived experience. The framework is drawn from affect heuristics. The affect heuristic influences how people predict their future emotions and make decisions based on those predictions. This process, known as affective forecasting, involves anticipating how future events will make us feel and so gives us internal insight, so to speak, which can support us to both deepen and refine our thinking for different life events based on our experiences (Finucane et al., 2000).

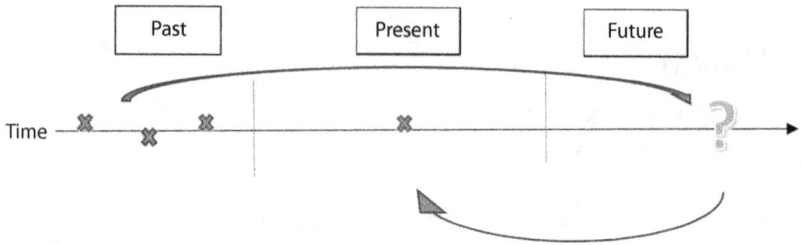

Past, present and future framework

(Created by Jordan Savage)

We all often find that our past experiences are being used to predict the future, which inevitably impacts our decisions and circumstances in the present – that piece of advice a parent always gave, the experiences we have had of different relationships (good or bad), the tips given on where the best place to do your shopping is and so on. The same principle can also be utilized in applying theory to our thinking in practice about the people we work with. For example, those experiences (past) of the interactions between a mother and her daughter and their impact on the developing child's predictions (future) about the safety of the world may become the internal working models and attachment styles (present).

Reflective thought

How could you apply this framework to your own life? Think of a situation that occurred in the past that you feel is influencing your decision-making now and your future decision-making? Do you think you could apply this in your practice?

If we take the notion that we use our experiences to predict the future and say those future predictions are drawn from trauma, loss and adversity, then consider what lies in wait in the now? How do we offer hope for the future and dilute these experiences of adversity with new positive experiences of change?

Applying the principles outlined above: a practice example.

Below is an example of how an evidence-based (knowledge and research) approach and theory contributed to direct work with a care experienced adult:

Whilst supporting a young man develop his independence, he was able to recall moments within his younger life, that to me displayed ability for motivation, planning, confidence and presenting skills within a public domain to an audience. This was mixed in with his recollections of the challenges and adversity he had experienced. It would appear in those early conversations that positive notions were difficult to imagine. In this scenario, person-centred approaches, utilising theory drawn from Solution Focussed Brief Therapy was utilised. In particular 'resource activation' and 'competency talk' were applied, (Shennan, 2020) these approaches enabled me to highlight the positive aspects observed directly back to him. This was further complimented by exploring 'relationship / noticing questions', which drew upon how others may have seen him using these skills in a moment of confidence, to develop alternative perceptions (George et al., 1999; de Jong & Berg, 2008).

Utilising client language appeared to make the greatest impacts upon outlooks, as he heard my comment of talent 'talent', which led to assertion being made that he didn't like this term as it implies, he was born with something, rather than acknowledges the hard work he had put into learning and developing the skills, (I loved this response from him). This was validated back, acknowledging he did indeed appear to have the ability to learn skills and work hard at learning things, with a wondering whether these abilities could be utilised for other aspects of life. This appeared to be a poignant turn of phrase, as he asked if this discussion could be sent to him days later via text, feeling this was a source of motivation. This draws upon hidden truths and standpoints being validated and therefore offering opportunities for reauthoring within the social context of language (White, 1995; O'Connell, 2012).

You can see from this example that whilst in the early sessions, his past experiences (X's in the timeline) had a part to play in predicting the future, therefore, affecting his here and now. Hidden resources have been activated from how he had previously developed a skill, and he has reauthored (some of the X's in the time line) and considered a new perspective, and so more positive predictions of the future develop, drawing his own motivations in the present. The young man in question, with his rediscovering of his strengths and motivations, did very well, and after years of struggles, he found his way to live well and independently. We can get some sense that there was time spent understanding the past of an individual, not just to understand the adversity experienced but also to understand the forgotten moments of success and amplify these as a resource to enable more optimistic predictions of the future. The roots here developed buds of change . . . one small step at a time. Davies and Gray (2017) highlight in their model (that has been adapted below) the individual's insight, knowledge and values – their expertise is the lens by which other types of knowledge are either included or excluded. This perhaps affirms that the concept of the application of theory, research and methods works in tandem with the developing understanding of the preferences of those with lived experience – their history, values, aspirations and environment where they live.

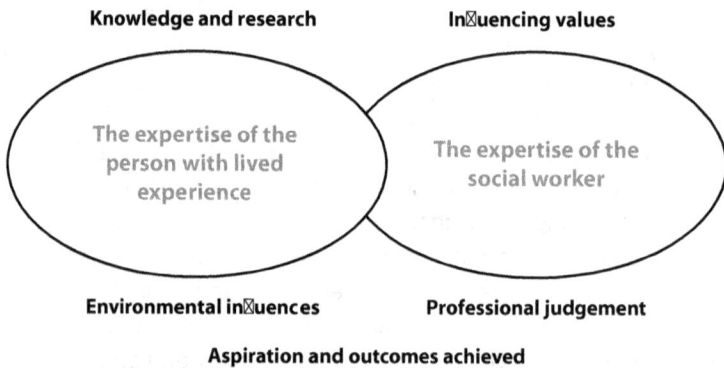

Knowledge and research	Influencing values
The expertise of the person with lived experience	The expertise of the social worker
Environmental influences	Professional judgement

Aspiration and outcomes achieved

The model above is similar to that of Davies and Gray (2017) but has been adapted to reflect, firstly, different terminology but to also highlight aspirations in addition to outcomes and to include professional judgement as the factors highlighted play a role in the judgements made.

Applying theory of the 'use of self'

The above examples are mostly fictitious but reflect the real practice of a social work apprentice. The examples have not only highlighted how theory and specialist knowledge can be applied in practice but have evidenced the importance of having the skill to be able to apply them appropriately. It is important to fully understand the reasons for why we may use different theory or evidence-based knowledge to inform decision-making.

If we take a moment to look back at the recent practice example, the use of reflective journalling would have been a useful method in supporting the apprentice learner's thinking of the young man's position and thinking. Reflection in social work practice – and in all practice where you are working with people with lived experience – is really impactful in supporting you to understand yourself, the decisions you make and how you could further enhance your learning and practice; the concepts of reflection are explored in detail in Chapter 7. The use of reflective journalling helps you to consider the relationship between yourself and the person with lived experience and supports you to consider what 'self' you are taking into the interactions you have. It is important to understand how being self-aware can support us to better interact with those we work with. Hennessey (2011) suggests that before we try to connect with the feelings of those we are supporting, it is important to have an understanding of how the 'self' interplays with others who may be experiencing distress, anger and feelings of despair. Miller (2006), cited in Hennessey (2011), further suggests that if those working with people do not have this core understanding, there is a danger of responding to our own needs rather than responding to the needs of those with lived experience effectively.

Social workers apply the 'use of self' in their practice by integrating their personal attributes, experiences and self-awareness into their professional interactions. Self-awareness is crucial, as it helps social workers understand how their personal experiences and feelings might influence their interactions with clients (Trevithick, 2018). Reflective practice enables social workers to critically evaluate their interactions and decisions, fostering continuous improvement (Gordon & Dunworth, 2017).

Critically evaluating our own interactions is essential. For one, it enables us to hold onto our professional boundaries, which protect both the person with lived experience and the worker, ensuring ethical practice (Kaushik, 2017). By drawing on your own personality, values and life experience, interventions are more genuine and relatable, therefore effectively becoming instruments of change (Kaushik, 2017); furthermore, being more in tune with your 'self' through self-awareness results in improved cultural awareness, which will result in you working in an anti-oppressive way consistently. The concept of self-awareness is explored in greater detail in other chapters, in particular Chapters 7 and 9. The activities integrated into these chapters will help you to consider the impact of self-awareness, which will support you to bring your 'self' to direct practice.

Case study from a former apprentice: exploring the theme of applying psychosocial theory and specialist knowledge to practice

From a personal perspective, in the whole time that I have spent in social care, I am yet to meet anyone that isn't in this type of work who doesn't want to be a force for good for others, but in the same rhetoric, I can say the same that all tend to have a narrative of how their own challenges or the challenges of those they care for had driven them to the role they now serve. This has been acknowledged within studies by Straussuer et al. (2018), who consider the notion of *'wounded healers'* and find, within surveys of social workers, that 40 per cent of respondents reported mental health problems prior to commencing their social work profession. Jung (1966) conceptualized the notion of the wounded healer based upon the Greek myth of Chiron, who overcame the pain of injuries to become a master healer, thus being put forwards by Jung under the notion that those who have experienced adversity are best positioned to understand the causes of others' anguish. This is something that you, no doubt, will explore within your apprenticeship when being introduced to psychosocial theories.

Identifying your own roots into the social work profession and assessing your real self can be an uncomfortable exercise; to reassure you, you can present as much or as little as you feel comfortable with in doing the exercise, but this deep reflection was one of the most valuable exercises of my time in the social work degree apprenticeship programme. To come full circle to some degree, whilst we may use a past, present and future framework in understanding others, this can be a useful exercise to consider the parallels in working with others to appreciate aspects of our own 'self' within those moments we share with the people we work with.

To draw upon this concept takes practice, and in particular, a useful tool for me was reflective journalling. You will find a way that suits you the best. I also felt it helpful to draw upon the notion of empathic imagination. Imagining, you could argue, is constructed from what we know about the person we work with and meshed with our own experiences (Gaesser, 2013). Research will inevitably support your wider practical work with those you are supporting.

For example, in considering my work as an apprentice social worker with adult care leavers, it was important to understand what challenges there were, both on the outside and those impacting me on an interpersonal level too. In researching the specific area, I found out a lot more that supported my practice; for example, I discovered that care leavers are at a higher risk of custody, exploitation, social exclusion and death in early adulthood, (Greenwood, 2017). Further research by Centrepoint (2017) found that 26 per cent of care leavers had sofa surfed whilst 14 per cent had slept rough since leaving care. Within Allain's (2016) study of care leavers, I found that those with the skills to access housing support and positively transition into independent living correlated with strong support from leaving care services through advocacy and negotiating outcomes. As a result of ascertaining this additional knowledge, I became more confident in the work I was doing.

You can therefore see that whilst it may give us a good feeling when we view a young person develop motivation and achieve good positive outcomes, this may also be met with the challenges of the system and the adversity experienced. In this case, then, we are applying theory, knowledge and research collectively in order to plan, assess and develop our interventions and approaches in order to then develop empowerment, opportunity and, ultimately, protection.

Before this chapter reaches its conclusion, it is useful to include a reminder about the range of support and resources available to you to support you to develop your confidence in applying theory to practice. Two useful and contemporary sources are detailed below in the recommended reading. Bassot's (2024) book in particular has a large number of activities and templates that you may find useful. Below is a template you could use with each intervention you undertake in order to support your thinking about the reason you are seeking an explanation, the reason you have thought about the theories you have, how much you understand the theories you have selected, how you can apply them and what they then tell you about the situation you have been questioning.

Reflective activity 4.3

The What?

The context of the situation and why you are questioning it.

| The event / intervention / piece of work / situation (give a brief description). | What is making me question this? (Think about the reasons why you have stopped to think? Was there something about someone's response? Was there something you couldn't explain? |

The Why?

Identifying the theory and considering its relevance – will you apply the chosen theories selected?

| What theories might be relevant to support you to understand the situation better? | What do you understand about the theories? Why are they relevant? Which part of them are the most relevant and why? |

The Application

Consideration of different perspectives and what the theory tells you.

| Are there other perspectives on the selected theories that may support you to understand the situation in a clearer way? | How can you apply the selected theories? What are they telling you about the situation? |

Chapter summary

This chapter has introduced you to different ways of thinking when it comes to applying social work theory and knowledge to practice. On the surface, it may appear and certainly feel like the concept of applying theory to practice is a complex task; however, once you begin to learn about the range of theory applicable to social work, you have the unique opportunity of being able to apply your new learning in the workplace, and so your off-the-job training can be translated through your usual on-the-job activities. Whilst this chapter has explored the experiences of a former social work apprentice and has considered different practice examples, whereby theory has been essential to understanding the experiences of those with lived experience, it can still be somewhat challenging to think about how the content of this chapter relates to our practice. It takes time to fuse the two concepts together and even more time to feel confident about applying theory to practice.

It is normal to feel a little anxious about choosing the right theories, and the reality of many social worker's practice is that, sometimes, it is trial and error in the sense that it may take a number of theory searches before you find one that really 'fits'. Additionally, given each person's experience is very different, sometimes, whilst you may find the same theories apply to many of the people you are working with, it may be that different parts of the same theories apply, and this is something else that takes some testing. What will become apparent as you work through the other chapters of this book is that the other skills you will develop along your journey, such as reflective and critical thinking skills, will further support you to cement the skill of applying theory to practice.

Recommended reading

There are many books that act as a good reference guide to supporting you to develop your knowledge base of social work; there are even books that specifically look at social work theory and the application of theory to practice. Here are some contemporary sources that have been referred to in this chapter that you may find useful.

Bassot, B. (2024). *Applying social work theory: A journal*. Bloomsbury Publishing.
Howe, D., & Hill, D. (2024). *A brief introduction to social work theory: Second edition*. Bloomsbury Publishing.

References

Allain, L. (2016). *The involvement of young people leaving care in social work education and practice*. DProf Thesis: Middlesex University.
Bowlby, J. (1988). *A secure base: Parent-child attachment and healthy human development*. Basic Books.

Buckner, R. L. (2010). The role of the Hippocampus in prediction and imagination. *Annual Review of Psychology, 61*(1), 27–48. https://doi.org/10.1146/annurev.psych.60.110707.163508.

Bretherton, I. (1993). From dialogue to internal working models: the co-construction of self relationships. In C. A. Nelson (Ed.), *Memory and affect in development: Minnesota symposia on child psychology* (Vol. 26). Lawrence.

Centrepoint. (2017). *From care to where? Care leavers' access to accommodation.* Centrepoint. https://centrepoint.org.uk/media/2035/from-care-to-where-centrepoint-report.pdf (accessed 07 September 2024).

Davies, K., & Gray, M. (2017). The place of service-user expertise in evidence-based practice. *Journal Of Social Work, 17*(1), 3–20.

De Jong, P., & Berg, I. K. (2008). *Interviewing for solutions* (3rd edn). Thompson Higher Education.

Fahlberg, V. (1991). *A childs journey through placement.* BAAF.

Finucane, M. L., Alhakami, A., Slovic, P., & Johnson, S. M. (2000). The affect heuristic in judgments of risks and benefits. *Journal of Behavioral Decision Making, 13*(1), 1–17.

Gaesser, B. (2013). Constructing memory, imagination, and empathy: a cognitive neuroscience perspective. *Frontiers in Psychology, 3*, 576. https://doi.org/10.3389/fpsyg.2012.00576.

George, E., Iveson, C., & Ratner, H. (1999). *Problem to solution* (2nd edn). BT Press.

Gordon, J., & Dunworth, M. (2017). *The use of self.* Oxford Academic.

Greenwood, G. (2017). *Early deaths among care leavers revealed.* BBC News. https://www.bbc.co.uk/news/uk-38961818 (accessed 07 September 2024).

Hennessay, R. (2011). *Relationship skills in social work.* Sage.

Howe, D., & Hill, D. (2024). *A brief introduction to social work theory: Second edition.* Bloomsbury Publishing.

HM Government. (2018). *Working together to safeguard children: A guide to interagency working to safeguard and promote the welfare of children.* HMSO.

Jung, C. G. (1928). *Contributions to analytical psychology* (H. G. Baynes & C. F. Baynes, Trans.). Kegan Paul, Trench, Trübner & Co.

Jung, C. G. (1966). *The practice of psychotherapy* (2nd edn). Bollingen Foundation.

Kaushik, A. (2017). Use of self in social work: Rhetoric or reality. *Journal of Social Work Values and Ethics, 14*(1), 21–9.

Miller, L. M. (2005). *Counselling skills for social work.* SAGE Publications. Available from: ProQuest Ebook Central [17 June 2019].

O'Connell, B. (2012) *Solution-focused therapy* (3rd edn). SAGE.

Rolfe, G., Freshwater, D., & Jasper, M. (2001). *Critical reflection in nursing and the helping professions: A user's guide.* Palgrave Macmillan.

Schacter, D. L., Addis, D. R., & Buckner, R. L. (2008). Episodic simulation of future events: Concepts, data, and applications. *Annals of the New York Academy of Sciences, 1124*(1), 39–60. https://doi.org/10.1196/annals.1440 .001.

Sheridan, M., Frost, M., & Sharma, A. (1997). *From birth to five years: Children's developmental progress* (New ed. / revised and updated by Marian Frost and Ajay Sharma). Routledge.

Shennan, Guy. (2020). Towards a Critical Solution-Focused Practice? *Journal of Solution Focused Practices*, 4, 15–21.

Straussner, S. L. A., Senreich, E., & Steen, J. T. (2018). Wounded healers: A multistate study of licensed social workers' behavioral health problems. *Social Work (New York), 63*(2), 125–33.

Thomas, G. (2017). *How to do your research project: A guide for students in education and applied social sciences* (3rd edn). Sage.

Trevithick, P. (2018). The 'self' and 'use of self' in social work: A contribution to the development of a Coherent theoretical framework. *The British Journal of Social Work, 48*(7), 1836–54.

Watson, J. B., & Rayner, R. (1920). Conditioned emotional reactions. *Journal of Experimental Psychology, 3*(1), 1–14.

White, M. (1995). *Re-authoring lives: Interviews and essays.* Dulwich Centre Publications.

5

Safeguarding and ethical practice

Laura James and Gemma Hunt

Chapter Outline

What apprentices can do to stay safe   82
Managing professional boundaries   84
Safe use of social media   87
Safeguarding in the social work context   89
Assessing and managing risk   90
Dealing with ethical tensions in practice   93
Professional judgement   96
Chapter summary   97

This chapter will unpack the concept of safeguarding from two different perspectives. Firstly, this chapter will support you to think about how you can keep yourself safe as a social work apprentice and will encourage you to think about the knowledge you need to keep yourself safe whilst in the workplace and in the university setting; for example, the chapter will explore professional boundaries and online safety in detail. The second part of the chapter will support you to better understand what is meant by the term safeguarding in the context of social work. This part will aid you in developing your knowledgebase around safeguarding and will explore the notion of ethical practice and value-based social work. Whilst this chapter cannot go into great detail about child and adult specific safeguarding topics, the chapter will give you the tools to be able to think about the critical lens required to explore the tensions surrounding safeguarding practice in context; these should prove useful to you when you undertake the specialist safeguarding related modules in university. This chapter will include a range of reflective exercises, and there will be some top tips included too.

When you think about social work and the term 'safeguarding', it may that you automatically think about it from a practice perspective and from the perspective of keeping vulnerable individuals safe from harm. As a social work apprentice and indeed as an individual on the journey to qualification, it is important to be mindful about how you safeguard yourself too. On your journey to becoming to a qualified social worker, being mindful of your well-being, your personal safety and your personal and professional boundaries will ensure that you can practice in a way that is safe. This isn't to say that just because you will be mindful of the above that things will always go smoothly, as this unfortunately will not always be the case; however, being mindful of how you safeguard yourself will ensure you are as prepared for study and practice as possible and that you will have or know where to find the strategies that will help you look after yourself. Chapter 9 focuses specifically on how you can manage your well-being, and so whilst the idea of well-being will be referenced in this chapter, you will find much greater detail, top tips and an abundance of strategies to help you manage your well-being in Chapter 9.

What apprentices can do to stay safe

The term safety can mean different things to different people, so it is important to be aware of what safety means to you and to be mindful of your early warning signs as you go about your work as a social work apprentice. For those of you who have come across or completed protective behaviours training, you might be familiar with the term early warning signs and the importance of tuning into those things we experience when we feel unsafe. The Protective Behaviours (PB) process explains how our bodily changes, such as butterflies in our stomach and feeling uneasy on our feet (wobbly knees), are indicators that we do not feel okay in this situation (PB Association, 2017). If you experience your early warning signs, it is important not to ignore these and to consider what action you might need to take. The protective behaviours process is a practical and empowering approach to personal safety, which considers the importance of trusting our intuitive feelings (early warning signs). If this is the first time you have come across the PB process, you are encouraged to visit the PB Association website to develop your knowledge further.

There may be many occasions where you have experienced your early warning signs, including in the workplace, in the community and at university. When we begin to think about the number of areas where we may encounter feeling unsafe, we start to see several areas of potential concern, especially when we consider the work that social workers do. They undertake home visits, work with people in the community and respond to concerns raised about the safety of children and / or vulnerable adults. That is not to say all aspects of social work are dangerous or risky, but there are occasions where, as professionals, we may need to take proactive steps to keep ourselves safe.

Before we move on to consider some of the precautions you may want to think about, it is important to mention that most visits to families and people at home will be completely safe, and more often than not, you will be met and treated with respect (Cooper, 2012). There will be times, however, particularly in safeguarding work, where you may be viewed as a threat and as someone who has a lot of power. When people feel vulnerable and frightened, their behaviour may become more hostile or resistant in your presence. If you encounter a situation where you begin to experience your early warning signs, the following top tips are useful actions to consider:

Top tips

- When you visit a family at home, remember this is their private space. Always be respectful, considerate and polite. As a social work apprentice, you will likely encounter lots of occasions where you may need to have difficult conversations; remaining respectful will help to reduce the likelihood of escalation. You will need to also consider who you are visiting. Do you know the family? Are there any markers to indicate someone may present a risk to professionals?
- Think about where you sit; try to sit near a door. Can you see the person you are visiting at all times? Also, be aware of everyone in the property. Do you know your way out of the property; is the exit clear? If you do start to experience your *early warning signs* at any point, find a way to exit the property. If you feel uneasy at all, listen to your instincts, and leave when it is safe to do so.

- Lots of families have pets; you should consider this carefully and think about where you sit on this continuum. Some social workers set out clearly to all families that they do not like animals and that large dogs can feel especially intimidating. However, others really like animals and very much see them as part of the family. At times, showing kindness and patience towards animals can put families at ease; they may find their pets a comfort during your visit. However, if you feel uncomfortable about animals, respectfully request they are placed in a different room.
- Always make sure your manager and / or colleagues know your whereabouts and expected time of return. Some teams have a buddy system where they message when they are going into a property, especially if the family is unknown and there are worries around potential risk. If you are working from home and going out to complete visits, again, make sure you stay in contact with your team; your safety is a priority.
- Think about travelling in advance. Will you be visiting a family in your car? If so, make sure you know where you are going and park in the direction you intend to leave. Make sure you have easy access to your car keys and park close by if possible. If you are using public transport, make sure you have planned your route and, wherever possible, visit during daylight.
- A final consideration is your location and using the office or community-based spaces to undertake assessments or discussions when you know there are potential risks. If you have any worries that a person is dangerous or may pose a risk, asking them to attend the office is a way of managing such difficulties. It is also important to have a second worker present and, again, consider the positioning of where you sit – you should sit near the door. Most offices also have panic alarms built in as a precaution.

Managing professional boundaries

Professional boundaries can be understood as a set of expectations or rules that set the ethical standards within a given profession (Cooper, 2012). In social work, the professional standards set by Social Work England outline what a 'social worker must know, understand and be able to do' (SWE, 2025). This includes promoting people's rights, maintaining trust and confidence, acting safely, respectfully and with professional integrity – all of which require us to uphold professional boundaries. In short, boundaries underlie almost everything we do within social work; this is how we ensure a safe, professional and supportive response. Upholding key boundaries not only protects us as social workers but also protects the people we work with.

Given the range of tasks social workers undertake, there is not a one-size-fits-all guide when it comes to managing boundaries. There are so many different situations and circumstances which could arise, that it would be near-impossible to capture them all here. So, if you do find yourself in a situation where you are unsure about something, ensure you seek guidance from your manager. There are, however, some key areas that you should hold in mind as a social work apprentice as you go about your day-to-day work with people and their families.

Firstly, a key aim of professional standards and guidelines is to ensure that the relationship between a social worker and those accessing services is kept on a *professional* level and does not develop into a personal relationship – or is perceived by others as a personal relationship (Cooper, 2012). Whilst social workers do indeed have to be 'friendly' towards people they are supporting, being friendly is not the same as becoming someone's friend (Ward, 2018). As a social work apprentice, you will be expected to demonstrate warmth, compassion and understanding but should not expect this in return. Likewise, as part of your work, there will be times when those with lived experience ask about your personal circumstances. For example, many of the students and apprentices we work with often get asked if they have children, whether they are married, their age, etc. The way you respond to such questions will likely depend on several factors (appropriateness, relevance and safety for example), which you will need to consider when determining how to respond.

Whilst social workers do need to relate to those with lived experience, they will need to make a number of decisions about what to share, when to share and whether this is in-keeping with the professional task and boundaries set. Equally, as a social work apprentice, you will also encounter situations where you will need to carefully consider how much you share about yourself. Thinking about and exploring the *use* of self is complex; you are required to make conscious decisions about what to share and why (Ward, 2018). To manage boundaries, it is important to set out clear parameters when you begin to work with a person or family; explaining the boundaries can help those you are supporting and workers to understand their respective roles. At times, you may need to support people to implement boundaries and perhaps act as a role model for others when needed. Furthermore, upholding boundaries around time management, managing emotions and behaviours, and being respectful around diversity and equality are key to building safe relationships. You may find some of the content and activities in Chapter 7 helpful in supporting you to think about the use of self.

A further area we would like to highlight, which is likely to be tested at some stage in your social work journey, is around physical contact. Now, your immediate response here might be a hard no, that physical contact is a professional boundary you will not cross. If this is the case, you are not alone in this response; many social workers will share this view. However, physical contact is often seen as being on a continuum and dependent on the situation and circumstances. Below is a case example for you to consider and discuss with your workplace mentor during supervision.

Case example 1:

You have arranged to see a young child in school. During the session, they become upset and tearful during a piece of life story work and try to seek comfort and reassurance from you. This is a tricky situation for you because on the one hand, you strongly believe that physical contact should be avoided (this is a professional boundary), but on the other hand, you believe that a child who is grieving for their family should receive some level of comfort – perhaps an arm around the shoulder. Before you go ahead and offer any level of physical contact (even if you believe this is needed) what other factors should you consider? Write a list of the things that might influence your decision.

- Did you consider the child's age and stage of development?
- Did you consider the child's gender and culture?
- Did you consider the child's history and any incidents of harm and / or abuse?
- Did you consider the need to ask the child for consent to offer physical contact?
- Did you consider the impact of not providing any physical contact?
- Did you consider whether the child may have a disability or learning difficulty?
- Did you consider whether the child's need for comfort outweighed your boundary around physical contact?
- Did you think about your own safety and risks of allegations?
- Did you consider your own gender and whether this could impact how others perceive this physical contact?
- Did you consider how others would feel if they saw you put your arm around a child's shoulder to comfort them?

Whilst this list is not exhaustive, it highlights how much you may need to consider and weigh up in just one decision around boundaries.

By developing a greater understanding of professional boundaries and how to navigate these in your practice, you will be working towards achieving the following two occupational duties:

Duty 4: Establish and maintain the trust and confidence of people so as to develop professional relationships that ensure they understand the role of a social worker in their lives.

Duty 6: Work directly with individuals and their families through the professional use of self, using interpersonal skills to develop relationships based on openness and transparency.

Safe use of social media

Information and communication technology has grown considerably during the past decade, and since the pandemic, social workers and wider professionals have had to respond quickly to the changing nature of how we use technology in social work. This, of course, includes the use of social media. Social media is a broad term, which is often used to describe communication and social interaction across a wide range of platforms and is typically associated with social networking sites like Facebook, X (formally Twitter) and LinkedIn (Jackson, 2019). The Scottish Social Services Council (2017) has defined social media as the 'online platforms you use to engage – to create relationships, have conversations and communicate with others' (SSSC, 2017). It is a virtual platform where you can upload content, often about yourself, family and friends; and with the rise in the use of digital technologies, including smartphones and tablets, posting personal stories has never been so easy. With the increased use of social media tools, we have seen the introduction of multiple social media platforms, including WhatsApp, Instagram, TikTok, YouTube, Snapchat, Pinterest and Reddit, to name a few.

Whilst it is widely accepted that social media can be a supportive tool and a way to communicate and interact with an online community, Social Work England reminds us that social media sites are also public places (SWE, 2019). Under Standard 5.6, the regulator advises social workers to be cautious about what they post on social media and to refrain from posting anything that may 'damage confidence in their work, or the profession' (SWE, 2019). Within your role as a social work apprentice, you should ensure you are familiar with your organization's social media policies and should not post anything on social media that breaches your employer's code of conduct. When you are considering what to post on social media, it is important to think about confidentiality and refrain from posting comments about the people you support and your colleagues (SWE, 2019).

Returning to our previous discussion on professional boundaries, the same principles apply when interacting and communicating with people online. As a social work apprentice, you must maintain appropriate personal and professional boundaries in your working relationships with those with lived experience and colleagues (BASW, 2018). Whilst social media can be an effective way of breaking down communication difficulties and a useful way of reaching out to people, particularly those who struggle to share their views and feelings face-to-face, social workers are still required to uphold professional boundaries. It would not be appropriate, for example, to 'accept' those with lived experience or their carers as online 'friends' in a personal network (BASW, 2018).

Alongside maintaining professional boundaries, as a social work apprentice, you also need to consider your own safety when using social media. Given how easy it is to access personal information, you should consider how much of your *personal self* you wish to share on social media. Whilst for many of us, our offline and online worlds now often merge, the safeguards in the *real* world are not the same as in the *virtual* world, where things are instant – confidential information can be shared and traced at the click of a button (BASW, 2018). It is important, then, to check personal security settings on social media; this will help to keep your personal information private. Whilst the benefits of social media use are vast, social workers also need to know how to manage potential risks to their personal security, including their own friends and families (BASW, 2018; SSSC, 2017).

As a social work apprentice, you are required to develop knowledge and skills in using social media platforms, alongside other forms of information and communication technology. Whilst we have focused on social media here, in recent months, there has been an accelerated growth in the use of artificial intelligence (AI), which, again, is now being used more frequently in social work practice. This is a fast-changing landscape, so it is important to stay up to date with sector changes and your organizational policies, which will enable you to work towards meeting the following two occupational duties:

Duty 18: Social workers must use technology, social media or other forms of electronic communication lawfully, ethically and in a way that does not bring the profession into disrepute and ensure their skills in this area are maintained and used to improve practice.

Duty 19: Act safely, respectfully and with professional integrity; promote ethical practice; and report concerns.

Reflective activity 5.1

Pause here and think about your current social media use; what platforms do you regularly use, and how much information do you share? Do you share photos of friends and family? Can people access this personal information?

Now review your security settings; are any of your accounts 'open'? Can people see your friends lists or recent posts? Are you easy to find from your profile photo?

Do you have separate personal and professional social media platforms? Is there any crossover here? Do you allow your work colleagues access to your personal accounts?

What could you do differently to make yourself safer online?

Safeguarding in the social work context

Safeguarding is a very broad term that is given to the interventions required to keep someone safe, for example, a child, young person or adult. Everyone has a role to play when it comes to safeguarding, and the term 'intervention' in this context could mean a range of different things which could be undertaken by different people. The concept of safeguarding is shared by the 'values society holds around what is acceptable, or what is considered harm or danger and is shaped by our reflective social work practice over time' (Douglas and Fourie, 2022, pg. 7). As a social work apprentice, you will play a large part in 'safeguarding', and the work you do with those with lived experience will be underpinned by your organizational safeguarding policy that is shaped by wider governmental level policy and legislation. Thinking from a child and family social work position, the terms 'safeguarding' and 'child protection' are often used interchangeably in practice, and for you as apprentices, it can be difficult to understand the difference. Douglas and Fourie (2022) suggest that the 'distinguishing feature of the shift towards safeguarding is the concept of managing risk' (pg. 7).

To extend this further, it may be helpful to think of safeguarding as a proactive approach taken by organizations and individuals to prevent harm to those who may be at risk of it. In order to ensure robust safeguarding that is effective, your organization will have a policy that will detail the roles and responsibilities of everyone; it will include important information that seeks to increase the knowledge of those in the organization, and there will be a clear process to follow should safeguarding concerns arise. As a social work apprentice, likely working in an organization that seeks to safeguard those at risk of harm on a daily basis, you will be working within a more direct safeguarding remit, and your day-to-day work will focus on protecting those who are vulnerable through responding to safeguarding concerns rather than preventing them in the first place (this isn't to say that the preventative work hasn't taken place prior to the concern or that it doesn't follow after in the hope that a further concern isn't raised; however, the first response is often an intervention that seeks to address the concerns raised rather than prevent the concerns from occurring in the first place). When you think about the work of social workers in this way, you will likely see that they respond to safeguarding concerns that have been shared and seek to 'protect' children, young people and adults through a reactive approach rather than a proactive one; this in the context of children's social work, becomes child protection rather than safeguarding.

Assessing and managing risk

In much of your future practice as a qualified social worker, you will be tasked with assessing the risk posed to those you are working with, whether this be vulnerable children and young people or vulnerable adults in need of support. In order to be able to safeguard those with lived experience and react accordingly to the concerns that have been raised, assessing the level of harm will require robust assessment of risk and identification of protective factors. The term 'assessment' is recognized as a key task in social work (Parker, 2021), so much so that in the UK, there are a number of frameworks that have been developed specifically for assessment in social work; these frameworks seek to ensure that social workers are able to effectively investigate, plan and intervene appropriately so that positive outcomes are achieved for those who are being assessed (Parker, 2021).

Gathering information is the first part of assessing risk, and this can be done in a number of ways; for example, through communicating directly with those who have been identified as being at risk of harm and also family members, where appropriate. You will need to consider the needs of those you are working with and adapt your communication style to meet these needs; you may also need to be creative in your approach in order to ascertain the information you need to assess risk and support needs. Other means of information gathering are essential too, for example, speaking to other professionals who are either currently involved in the person's life or who have been previously. Reading case histories and accessing information about previous concerns and service engagement are vital as well. Once you have gathered all of the information required, you will begin your analysis in order to determine the level of risk, the degree of vulnerability and the number of protective factors present that may offer some mitigation. You will likely present your assessment findings and analysis in a specific assessment format.

When compiling your findings, it is important to think about the relevance of social work theory. In the previous chapter, the concept of application of theory to practice was examined, and a range of examples were given in relation to how theory can support the analysis of information so that you can better understand a situation. Some workplaces encourage explicit reference to theory and research in social work assessments, as, by providing an evidence-base, findings can be better presented and substantiated. Once the risk has been fully assessed, you will then be in a position where you can seek to manage the presenting risk.

Reflective activity 5.2

Think about a piece of work you have undertaken in the workplace recently, and consider the following questions:

- What informed your information gathering? Who did you speak to?
- Did you have enough information to assess risk effectively?

- When you were analysing the information you had sought, did you draw upon theory or research to inform your analysis? If you didn't, how do you think you could draw upon it to inform your future assessments?

As an apprentice, you will have lots of opportunities to assess risk and will be able to shadow and implement different means of managing risk in order to prevent harm or further harm to those who are vulnerable. Depending upon your prior experience and, indeed, where you are on your apprenticeship journey, the thought of identifying and managing risk may feel very frightening; however, you will be fully supported in the workplace to undertake these tasks, and this is how you will learn, develop and make progress against the social worker apprenticeship standard.

Encompassing a number of knowledge and skill statements from the apprenticeship standard are the following two occupational duties, both of which focus upon assessment completion and the intricacies involved in social work assessment. By developing your confidence in assessing and managing risk, you will develop competence in these duties.

Duty 9 Be accountable for quality practice and decisions made whilst working within legal and ethical frameworks, using professional authority and judgement appropriately and respectfully.

Duty 10 Select and use appropriate frameworks to assess, give meaning to, plan, implement and review effective interventions and evaluate the outcomes, in partnership with service users.

(IfATE, 2023)

To follow on from the point above, you may be wondering how you will be expected to assess risk and determine the support required for those who have been deemed to be at risk of harm. As you begin to develop your confidence in conducting assessments, you will be directed to a range of tools which will support you to identify and manage risk in your practice. Your organization will have bespoke tools that are used, and in addition to these, there are other tools available that can support you to assess concerns such as neglect in children and adults.

Reflective activity 5.3

Pause here and think about the tools available in your workplace that you and others are able to use to assess risk.

Think about the different concerns you may be presented with in a referral in your current workplace / team / placement setting. Undertake some research through using the internet, speaking to colleagues and exploring resources in your organization to identify the range of specialist tools that can support your assessment of risk.

Dealing with ethical tensions in practice

In a profession that is often portrayed by the media in a negative light, the complex nature of the social worker role continues to pose a challenge, yet there are so many like you who aspire to join the sector in order to seek to make that positive difference to people's lives. As a large part of the social worker role is about making decisions about people's lives, social workers are often presented with some complex ethical tensions. Social worker's values often play a part in ethical practice. The PCF as discussed in other chapters sets out nine domains detailing the knowledge and skills that you should be working towards in your social work training and beyond, one of which is named: values and ethics. During your studies, you will be taught about being aware of your own values and how these can differ from others. Your own personal values influence your professional values and how you apply ethical principles in your practice (McGregor, 2011). It is important to ensure that human dignity is kept at the core of social work practice and that decisions are made in the very best interests of those who require support.

BASW's code of ethics (2018) expects social workers to fully respect every human being in their own right and to ensure that each person in need of protection receives the protection they need. BASW (2018; pg. 4) states:

> Ethical awareness is fundamental to the professional practice of social workers. Their ability and commitment to act ethically is an essential aspect of the quality of the service offered to those who engage with social workers.

Respect for human rights and a commitment to promoting social justice are at the core of social work practice throughout the world.

Reflective activity 5.4

Spend some time reading through BASW's (2018) Code of Ethics for Social Work. This can be accessed here:
https://basw.co.uk/sites/default/files/resources/Code%20of%20Ethics%20Aug18.pdf

Prior to becoming a social work apprentice, you may not have heard of this code before. Take a look at the values and ethical principles and consider how you are or how you will adopt these in your practice.

In order to practice applying them, write a short 200-word reflective paragraph about an intervention you have recently carried out. Identify the values and ethical principles you applied during this intervention. This would be a useful piece to share in your next progress review and / or your next supervision session with your workplace mentor.

One of the most complex ethical tensions is that of rights versus responsibilities or care versus control. As social workers have a statutory responsibility to make decisions in the best interests of the person who is at risk of harm, social workers are often challenged by the impact of their decision-making, in that there could be significant changes imposed upon a person's life because of the professional judgement and overall decision made. There are legal implications that either determine or hinder actions taken, and quite often, social workers can feel really disheartened by the fact that they may feel they cannot proceed to take appropriate action that would seek to protect those in need because of legal challenges, capacity issues, financial constraints or a lack of resources compared to the level of need that is presenting. In the last decade and even prior to it, the sector has faced numerous cuts, and this has had an impact on social worker decision-making, resulting in social workers feeling unable, at times, to practice in an ethically sound way when, for example, an adult in need of support isn't able to have the package of care they really need and would benefit from because of budget constraints within the organization hindering the right decision.

Below is an example of an ethical tension in practice for you to think about.

Case example 2:

The context: A social worker has received a referral which suggests there are concerns for a child aged eight. The concerns suggest that the child is being neglected due to very poor home conditions, poor attendance at school, ill-fitting clothes and a reported lack of food in the home.

As the referral and the information gathered following the referral did not suggest that the child was at risk of significant harm, the response did not warrant a s.47 enquiry. The appropriate response would be to assess the family at a child in need (s.17) level.

The tension: The parents, who have parental responsibility for the child, have the right to consent to the assessment and the support that may follow. Or they could decide not to give their consent.

Article 8 of the Human Rights Act 1998 stipulates that a person has a right to a private family life, and so the social worker, whilst having a responsibility to assess and support, does not have the right to intervene due to their not being any concerns warranting a s.47.

This poses a challenge for the social worker, as whilst she is mindful of the responsibilities she has as a social worker, she is also mindful of the fact that legally, unless there was a much higher risk, she cannot impose any form of assessment or support; yet she is worried about the concerns raised and the needs of the child and would like the family to engage in an assessment so that they can be offered the right support. The family, however, are within their rights to decline all interventions at this point, meaning that the child may continue to live in the same way without the support required to make things better.

Reflective activity 5.5

Having read the example above, think about the reasons outlined in this section that may cause an ethical tension which relate to decision-making. Think about the context, the relevant legislation and policy where applicable, the value base of either yourself or a social worker and your overall thoughts and feelings.

Have you encountered something similar? How would you feel?

Professional judgement

As a social work apprentice, you will learn a lot about the use of professional judgement in practice and will develop your confidence in using your professional judgement to inform the decisions that you make. All decisions you make will be informed by professional judgement, and the professional judgement you use will be informed by a number of different things, such as legal frameworks, knowledge from other sources, ethical principles and even intuition. It is important to note here that whilst intuition often plays a role in professional judgement, it is deemed unethical to use it in isolation (Killick & Taylor, 2024). When assessing the level of risk in practice, in order to inform the judgements you make, you will likely use a threshold document or a specific criterion in order to inform your thinking about what level and form of protection should be provided; examples may include Working Together to Safeguard Children (Department of Education, 2023) or the Care Act 2014 (Killick & Taylor, 2024).

Over the last three decades, the concept of risk has become more of an issue within social work, and social workers have to continually ask the questions: is the risk high enough to warrant a statutory intervention; is there evidence that the risk posed will result in significant harm to the individual? Organizations have created models of practice to support social workers to be more risk focused in their practice whilst, in the same time period, there have been increasing challenges in society relating to risk awareness and risk aversion too; this has caused additional tensions in social work practice and the caring professions and has resulted in changing thresholds too. When thinking about the concept of risk and the use of thresholds in practice, it could be said that 'judgements made about whether a situation is above or below some threshold of risk or need may form the basis for choosing between 'care' and 'control' as a focus of action (Alfandari, Taylor & Baginsky et al. cited in Killick & Taylor, 2024: 119). As noted earlier on in this chapter, this may result in an ethical tension for a social worker, as solely relying upon a threshold to determine the course of protective action may result in missed opportunities to provide the support that those who are vulnerable need.

Some concerns that are more difficult to evidence, such as neglect, can pose a challenge to assess, and making judgements can be difficult using a threshold alone. Sometimes, the prior knowledge and experience of social workers is drawn upon to support the decision-making around complex issues such as neglect, and the idea of intuition in collaboration with other factors may be used to inform professional judgement. Thinking about the impact of bias is important in situations of uncertainty, and the need to be professionally curious is key too. Whilst the thought of professional judgement may feel frightening as a social work apprentice, it is important to remember that, legally, social workers are the ones responsible for making decisions, and during your time of learning as an apprentice, you will be given lots of opportunities to share your professional judgement in practice with your workplace mentor, using the knowledge and tools available to you to support you to develop this skill.

In developing your professional judgement skills, which will support the decisions you go on to make, you will be working towards achieving competencies against the apprenticeship standard, for example, the skill statement of 'respond appropriately to signs of harm, abuse and neglect' (S30, IfATE, 2023), and you will be working towards achieving the following two occupational duties, which encompass a large number of knowledge, skill and behaviour statements:

Duty 9: Be accountable for quality practice and decisions made whilst working within legal and ethical frameworks, using professional authority and judgement appropriately and respectfully.

Duty 12: Recognize the risk indicators of different forms of abuse and neglect and their impact on individuals, their families or their support networks and prioritize the protection of children and adults in vulnerable situations.

(IfATE, 2023)

Chapter summary

This chapter has sought to frame your thinking of safeguarding from two quite different positions. In exploring the concept of how you can keep yourself safe, you will now hopefully have a clearer idea of the challenges you may face in relation to your own safeguarding but also how you can manage these should they arise. The use of technology and online platforms is very much embedded in today's society, and how you manage the use of these is important. Recognizing how you conduct yourself and the impact of what happens in your personal life, too, is crucial. Being self-aware will support you in being able to keep your self safe, as will keeping your knowledge up to date of relevant issues that may be experienced or observed; for example, keeping up to date with the latest Prevent training is essential and will certainly form part of your apprenticeship training. Don't forget that in order to practise safely, managing your own well-being needs to be a top priority. As was mentioned in the introduction of this chapter, you can refer to the top tips and guidance in Chapter 9 to help you to make sure your well-being is managed effectively.

This chapter has considered what safeguarding means from a practice perspective and has examined the difference between safeguarding and protection. When working in a safeguarding or protection focused role, you will experience ethical tensions whereby you need to stop and pause and think about the impact of your own values on your practice; this chapter has provided some insight into working ethically and has provided some examples which will hopefully aid you in your practice both now and in the future as a social worker. Finally, this chapter has touched upon the concept of assessing and managing risk and the use of professional judgement, both of which you will develop and enhance during your apprenticeship journey in readiness to implement autonomously once you are qualified and registered as a social worker.

Recommended reading

BASW. (2018). *The code of ethics for social work*. https://basw.co.uk/sites/default/files/resources/Code%20of%20Ethics%20Aug18.pdf.

Cooper, F. (2012). *Professional boundaries in social work and social care*. Jessica Kingsley publishers.

References

BASW. (2018). *The code of ethics for social work*. https://basw.co.uk/sites/default/files/resources/Code%20of%20Ethics%20Aug18.pdf.

Cooper, F. (2012). *Professional boundaries in social work and social care*. Jessica Kingsley publishers.

Department for Education. (2023). *Working Together to Safeguard Children*. HM Government.

Douglas, V., & Fourie, J. (2022). *Safeguarding children, young people and families*. Learning Matters.

IfATE. (2023). *Social Worker Integrated Degree*. Accessible here: https://www .instituteforapprenticeships.org/apprenticeship-standards/social-worker -integrated-degree-v1-1

Jackson, R. (2019). *Social media and social service workers*. https://www.iriss .org.uk/resources/insights/social-media-and-social-service-workers.

Killick, C., & Taylor, B. J. (2024). *Assessment, risk and decision making in social work*. Learning Matters.

McGregor, K. (2011) *Ethical dilemmas for social workers at a time of cuts*. Community Care. https://www.communitycare.co.uk/2011/02/04/ethical -dilemmas-for-social-workers-at-a-time-of-cuts/.

Parker, J. (2021). *Social work practice*. Learning Matters.

Protective Behaviours Association. (2017). *What does 'protective behaviours' actually mean?* https://www.protectivebehaviours.org/what-does-protective -behaviours-mean.

Scottish Social Services Council. (2017). *Social media guidance for social service workers*. SSSC. https://hub.careinspectorate.com/media/1621/social-media -guidance-for-social-service-workers.pdf (accessed 19 January 2025).

Social Work England. (2019). *Professional standards guidance*. https://www .socialworkengland.org.uk/standards/professional-standards-guidance/ #technology.

Social Work England. (2025). *Professional standards*. https://www .socialworkengland.org.uk/standards/professional-standards/.

The British Association of Social Workers. (2018). *BASW policy social media*. https://basw.co.uk/sites/default/files/resources/Social%20Media%20Policy .pdf.

Ward, A. (2018). The use of self in relationship-based practice. In G. Ruch, D. Turney, & A. Ward (Eds.), *Relationship based social work* (pp. 55–74). Jessica Kingsley publishers.

6

Work-based learning
How to get the most out of workplace opportunities

Ian Browne and Laura James

Chapter Outline

Off-the-job and on-the-job training 103

Bridging the gap between off-the-job and on-the-job training 104

What opportunities may count as off-the-job training
(thinking from a work-based learning perspective)? 105

Documenting your new learning 107

Examples of work-based learning 108

Shadowing and observing 108

Interdisciplinary working 109

Learning from other apprentices 110

Engaging with feedback 110

Other work-based learning opportunities 112

Reflecting upon prior learning 113

Different frameworks at play 117

Different approaches to work-based learning 118

Evidencing your progress on placement 120

Will I be involved in determining work-based learning and
placement plans? 121

Using supervision and mentoring to further your learning   122
The team around you, the apprentice   123
Chapter summary   124

This chapter will focus specifically on the work-based element of the social work apprenticeship and will support you as an apprentice learner to think about how you can shape and get the most out of each opportunity afforded to you in the workplace. This chapter will encourage you to think about the different types of support available to you in the workplace, including the utilization of supervision. This chapter will further consider the relationship between the training provider and the employer and, crucially, the role of the workplace mentor. Finally, this chapter will explore the different approaches taken nationally to work-based learning, thinking also about the numerous frameworks at play, and will explore the difference between off-the-job and on-the-job training in detail. This chapter will include activities relating to maximizing work-based learning.

As noted in the introductory chapter, each apprentice learner's journey is very different, and this is largely due to the fact that social work apprentice learners work in different settings and teams across the country; as such, the opportunities available in the workplace will vary vastly. Some employers may be very experienced in the delivery of the social work apprenticeship; others may be quite new to the apprenticeship programme, and so the work-based opportunities available may be being developed during your apprenticeship journey. Whilst your employer, who is invested in your apprenticeship journey, will likely give you and signpost you to many exciting, challenging and stretching opportunities in the workplace to further your knowledge, skills and behaviours, it is also important that you take ownership over your own learning and seek out opportunities that will further your learning and development against the apprenticeship standard. As an apprentice, approximately 80 per cent of your working week is spent in the workplace; this is where you are learning on the job but also where you are likely going to be afforded additional off-the-job training opportunities which will supplement and scaffold the academic learning provided by your training provider. Quite often, it can be difficult to understand the difference between 'off-the-job' and 'on-the-job' training, and trying to depict what off-the-job training opportunities may comprise of can be equally as challenging.

This concept will be explored and recapped as follows, and further detail on the differences between on- and off-the-job can be found in both the introductory chapter and Chapter 3.

Off-the-job and on-the-job training

On-the-job training

On-the-job training is the training that you receive as an apprentice from your employer; this training enables you to do the role that you have been employed to do. As part of your current employed role, you will likely be afforded supervision and be able to access training and support so that you are able to fulfil your duties; this does not form part of the teaching and learning of the apprenticeship, which is largely carried out by the training provider (the university, in most cases). Whilst the knowledge, skills and behaviours will largely be taught by the training provider and in a classroom setting, you can apply the learning gained in the workplace during your on-the-job time. It is important that there is coherence between on-the-job and off-the-job training in order for your learning to be reinforced and embedded (IfATE, 2024).

Off-the-job training

The apprenticeship funding rules (23–4) as outlined by the Department for Education (2023: 5) state that:

> Off-the-job training is a statutory requirement for an English apprenticeship. The provider must verify that the off-the-job training delivered to the apprentice meets the following definition: It is training which is received by the apprentice within their practical period, during the apprentice's normal working hours, for the purpose of achieving the knowledge, skills and behaviours of the apprenticeship they are undertaking. By normal working hours we mean the hours for which the apprentice would normally be paid, excluding overtime.

The definition above refers to the importance of the relevance of off-the-job training activities to the apprenticeship standard being undertook. It is important that, firstly, all off-the-job training activities afforded to you as apprentice learners are relevant to the social worker role but also that the opportunities gradually increase in complexity in order to support you to enhance your knowledge of the social worker role and develop the skills required, thus, supporting you to become a confident and competent newly qualified social worker.

The minimum number of off-the-job training hours for a full-time apprentice learner is the equivalent of six hours per week. Your off-the-job training largely consists of your attendance to university and the engagement in learning during your time in the classroom; however, during the times when you are not in university, it is crucial that you maintain your off-the-job training, and this can be achieved in a number of ways, which will be explored shortly. It is key to say at this point, too, that you can record much more than the minimum six hours off-the-job training per week. Many social work apprentice learners are afforded opportunities in the workplace in addition to their university study day that enhance the occupational experience of the apprenticeship and provide the opportunity to apply the learning from the classroom into practice (as explored in Chapter 4). At the very beginning of your apprenticeship journey, it is encouraged that you ask your employer about the possible work-based off-the-job training opportunities available over the course of your apprenticeship, as it is worth thinking about how such opportunities could be accessed and planned in throughout your learning journey.

Bridging the gap between off-the-job and on-the-job training

Being on a social work apprenticeship programme places you in a unique position when it comes to work-based learning. All learners studying social work programmes have the opportunity to undertake practice placements, which are considered the most significant form of experiential learning, and the 'signature pedagogy' of social work as they allow learners to connect theory to practice and transfer their experience into professional knowledge and skills (Domakin, 2014; McSweeny & Williams, 2019). These experiences also allow learners to increase their confidence and shape their professional identity (Berrett-Abebe et al., 2023). When compared to your peers who are studying on other routes into social work, you will have an enhanced experience as you have the benefit of not only receiving placement type opportunities for selected periods of study, but you will also be exposed to experiential learning opportunities for much of the programme within the workplace through your on-the-job learning.

Although not necessarily considered work-based learning, you will also be afforded realistic assessments and experiential learning opportunities during your time studying through your training provider; these opportunities will complement the learning you undertake in the workplace. For example, some of the opportunities you may be exposed to are considered below:

- The use of authentic case studies which will promote learning from experience (Race, 2019).
- The use of realistic role-play activities, which provide a safe space to rehearse practice skills and increase self-awareness and reflection (Allemang et al., 2022).
- The involvement of 'experts by experience' to help facilitate teaching and provide feedback to support the development of skills such as communication and self-awareness (Skilton, 2011).
- Assessments in the form of placement portfolios, presentations and observations which require you to apply knowledge to real life practice situations.

Engaging in authentic teaching and assessment will allow you to carry out workplace learning and connect theory and practice within real life settings (Brown, 2019). When undertaking these different approaches to learning, you will be supported to make connections between the classroom and your own professional practice. Continuously being in a practice setting will ensure you are able to more readily make these connections, which will be advantageous to your whole learning experience.

What opportunities may count as off-the-job training (thinking from a work-based learning perspective)?

As suggested earlier, the opportunities you will be afforded will vary significantly, and not all apprentice learners will be given the same opportunities. It is important that the off-the-job activities you engage in reflect your developmental areas and that they align to the apprenticeship standard. Here are some examples that would count as off-the-job training for the social work apprenticeship standard in accordance with the current ESFA funding rules and off-the-job training rules:

- Engaging in learning through your training provider: the classroom learning you will attend delivered by your training provider (likely to be a university) seeks to support you to develop and enhance your knowledge of social work. As a result, each time you engage in this type of learning, it counts as off-the-job training. This type of learning will more than likely account for most of your recorded off-the-job training over the course of your apprenticeship.
- Shadowing in the workplace: if you are given opportunities to shadow social workers in the workplace and observe tasks that you haven't observed before and so promote your knowledge of the social worker role, this counts as off-the-job training.
- Attendance to training relevant to the social worker role: an example might be that you attend some training on assessment skills or trauma-informed practice. If the learning from the training aligns to the apprenticeship standard and your role as a social work apprentice, it can count as off-the-job training.
- Undertaking a task that you haven't undertaken before that aligns to the apprenticeship standard: an example could be that after a period of shadowing a social worker colleague, you are given the opportunity (under supervision) to carry out part of an assessment with a person with lived experience, or you might chair a multi-agency meeting. If these tasks are tasks that you haven't completed before and include new learning for you aligned to the apprenticeship standard, these can count as off-the-job training.

The expectation to engage in new and continuous learning as part of your off-the-job training extends to the periods known as half terms and the training provider summer break. It is important that you regularly engage in and record your off-the-job training during these times too.

You will likely seek guidance and support from your training provider and employer, who can support your continuous learning in a number of ways during these periods. Examples of support may include:

- Support completion of assigned educational tasks set by your training provider.
- The creation of new learning opportunities in the workplace.

- Assigned research projects which benefit the development of you and the wider work force.
- Facilitating new shadowing opportunities, such as time spent in a new team to learn more about the remit and context of the team.
- Facilitating and creating opportunities to reflect on any new learning.

There are lots of different examples that will count as off-the-job training. It is important that you explore opportunities with your workplace mentor regularly in order to ensure that you are both maintaining your off-the-job training but also to ensure that you are taking up the additional opportunities in the workplace as every additional opportunity to further enhance your confidence and allow you to make good progress on your apprenticeship at a good pace.

Documenting your new learning

During your apprenticeship you are expected to complete a form of learner record (this could vary in format depending upon what software your training provider uses), which is a record of all new learning undertaken. An initial baseline assessment, currently known as a skill scan, is completed by you to assess and evaluate any learning undertaken prior to the programme, which helps formulate an initial plan, which is created in response to any learning needs identified. This activity is reviewed approximately every twelve weeks across the programme and provides evidence of your progression, competency and ability in respect of all KSBs. Progress reviews provide a forum to review your progress, map your learning and identify gaps in learning with suitable learning opportunities often being identified.

Top tip

- After each taught session or new learning experience in the workplace, get into the habit of recording your learning and map this against the apprenticeship KSBs. This will help you understand the apprenticeship much better and will also ensure that you are keeping on top of your recordings, which will support the compliance oversight that occurs within your apprenticeship.

Examples of work-based learning

There is a plethora of different learning opportunities which you can engage with in the workplace to help develop your skills, knowledge and competencies. All work-based learning will naturally align with the Professional Capabilities Framework (PCF), Social Work England's Professional Standards and the Apprenticeship Knowledge, Skills and Behaviours. Below are some examples across different domains of social work practice which can help you maximize learning and prepare for the challenges of professional practice.

Shadowing and observing

Shadowing your colleagues will provide you with invaluable opportunities to learn and develop and, if targeted, can help build a solid foundation for your future social work career. Some useful advice would be to not only shadow a variety of interesting and complex social work interactions but to also spend time with as many different colleagues as possible, as this will give you exposure to different roles and specialisms, diverse approaches and techniques, and enhanced communication skills, which will ultimately enable you to identify best practices and shape your own professional identity.

In order to maximize these valuable learning opportunities, it is important that you prepare in advance; for example, you may want to research the role or tasks that you will be observing, such as the process of a Child Protection Conference, or you may want to consider the approaches, theories or models which inform the interventions you will be observing. It may seem obvious but actively observing either mentally (deliberate, considered and focused) or through using written notes will ensure you absorb key aspects of practice such as communication techniques and decision-making processes. These observations will inform questions which you should ask afterwards. For instance, you could seek clarity around why the person your observed approached a situation in a particular way. These new and complex experiences will naturally generate learning, so it is important to record written reflections so you can actively develop your own practice. Chapter 7 looks at ways in which you can develop your reflective skills, and so you may wish to refer to this chapter for further information. Finally, it will be helpful if you follow up your observations, which can be done by further research to help you develop a deeper understanding and develop knowledge in areas you may not have understood at the time. One step further on from shadowing is to actually co-work some cases and be involved in certain pieces of work, as this will give you more hands on experience, which, if managed appropriately, will be in a safe and supportive environment.

Interdisciplinary working

Interdisciplinary working naturally builds upon shadowing and observing but involves seeking these opportunities with different professions. It is important to broaden your perspective and learn about how other teams and professions operate, as learning from the expertise of others will build your own professional network, help you develop a holistic understanding of the needs of those in receipt of social work services and will allow you to develop awareness of their perspectives and processes, which will ultimately inform your practice. For example, learning about how a Probation Officer supports an offender could teach you valuable skills about motivational interviewing and help shape your approach when working with resistant clients.

To maximize your development, you should be proactively seeking these opportunities, perhaps by simply asking any new professionals you encounter within your work-based learning. Other strategies include engaging in multi professional case discussions, multi-agency training and participation in joint interventions. When observing other professionals, you must prepare by ensuring you understand the context of the observed practice such as case details, policy frameworks and the roles of other professionals. This can be developed further by following up and diving deeper after the event. A simple approach is to ask questions and seek clarity on their approach. For example, asking them about what theories inform their practice. Being a quiet observer may not always be appropriate, and there may be opportunity to actively participate by offering your own insight and perspective, which will help build your confidence.

Learning from other apprentices

Smith & Shaw (2022) helpfully suggest that apprentices can also seek work-based learning opportunities from each other. One of the most amazing things about the social work apprenticeship is the amount of experience present within the classroom setting, and so it makes sense to seek opportunities which enable you to tap into this expertise by developing relationships and sharing practice knowledge with your peers from other settings. With the right conditions and permissions in place, you could organize and spend time with a peer and learn from them in their respective practice setting.

Engaging with feedback

The Social Work England professional standards highlight the importance of receiving positive and critical feedback, stating that it can improve self-awareness and enable you to identify future learning (SWE, 2019: standard 4.1). By valuing the input of others, trust and respect is enhanced, which can improve relationships between you, your colleagues and clients. Seeking feedback from people with lived experience is important, as they can offer a distinctive perspective on both good- and poor-quality input from social workers in training (Beasley & Taplin, 2023). Opportunities to receive feedback from those with lived experience will be plentiful, and some opportunities whereby you can gather feedback might be following an observation, during an introductory visit, at the point of closure of involvement or following a specific intervention. It is important to not just collect feedback but to reflect and act upon the feedback received, as this will aid your learning and development. Engaging with feedback in a meaningful way should become part of your practice.

It is important to think about your feedback strategy, which will be specific and unique to the individuals you are seeking it from. It will be of no help if the feedback simply tells you that you did well. For it to help develop your practice, you need to understand what you have done well and how you could improve your practice in the future (Beverley & Worsley, 2007). You also need to ensure that what you are asking is clear and understandable, particularly when working with those who may not understand what it is you are seeking, and so creative methods may be needed (Showell & Kerr, 2015). Before seeking feedback from those with lived experience, you may wish to consider the following questions to help plan your feedback strategy:

- Methods: what tools or approaches will you use? (e.g. informal conversations, feedback forms, creative methods like drawing or storytelling)
- Barriers: what challenges might you face in obtaining feedback? How will you try to overcome these?
- Ethics and Sensitivity: how will you ensure the feedback process is respectful and empowering for these clients? How will you address the power imbalance to ensure clients feel safe providing honest feedback?

Feedback should also be sought from colleagues, who may share written and verbal feedback about their experiences of working with you. Some of you will be well-established and experienced staff members within your organization, and so the notion of receiving honest and critical feedback can be more difficult due to these pre-existing relationships and power dynamics. It is important to consider how this can be addressed when seeking feedback. Your workplace mentor should be suitably placed to support you with this.

There are a variety of other ways you can look to obtain feedback during work-based learning. You will have regular supervision with your workplace mentor during your apprenticeship, and this protected time will often encompass feedback that seeks to support your learning and development. There will also be times where you are observed in practice, both formally and informally, and seeking feedback following these observations will shape your future practice. Furthermore, the feedback you will receive from your training provider in the classroom, within your progress reviews and from your peers will also influence your learning and development and be valuable to the progress you make in the workplace.

In order to maximize feedback opportunities during your work-based learning, it is important to be proactive. Seek feedback following challenging situations or tasks, which could generate learning for you. It will help if you reflect on these experiences yourself, as this will help prepare you for feedback discussions. It can be difficult receiving criticism, but try to view this positively as an opportunity to grow and develop as a practitioner and future social worker.

Other work-based learning opportunities

The following are other examples of work-based learning opportunities that you may wish to think about.

Opportunity	Examples	Benefits	How to maximize?
Participating in assessments	Gathering information from professionals for a Child and Family Assessment. Reflect on how decisions are made within a Mental Capacity Assessment.	Learn through observation, and develop core social work skills such as analysis and critical thinking. Improved understanding of the application of policy and legislation. Confidence can build in a safe environment.	Prepare and practice and make sure to ask questions. Reflect on the experience, and link your learning to standards and frameworks. Seek and act upon feedback.
Courses and training	Mental Health Awareness could teach you about different conditions, stigma and application of legislation. Prevention training could help you identify and support individuals vulnerable to radicalization	Enhances knowledge and skills. Increases confidence in subject area. Improves practice.	Work with your manager and support network to ensure CPD time is protected. Be proactive and seek these opportunities. Identify your own learning needs, and seek training in response. Reflect on your learning.
Engage in reflective practice	Attendance at peer group supervision to reflect and learn with others. Completion of reflective logs, which provide structure and aid critical reflection	Builds resilience as you will feel more in control of complex situations. Decision-making will be improved, as alternative perspectives will be considered	Make use of structured reflective models Be open to feedback, as this will give you new insights. Engage in written reflection so learning is recorded

This list is by no means exhaustive, as there is an abundance of specific learning opportunities which you can explore, and the important thing is that they are relevant to you and your own learning journey. Hopefully, these points help to highlight that there is always learning to be gained within the workplace. These opportunities can be maximized by preparing, practising, asking questions, engaging with feedback and reflecting to ensure you continually develop your knowledge and skills in the workplace.

Reflecting upon prior learning

Apprentice learners often commence the apprenticeship with substantial experience in relevant fields and sometimes with prior academic experience, too; therefore, it is crucial that you reflect upon your prior learning in order to shape the learning opportunities over the course of your apprenticeship. Reflecting upon what knowledge and skills you may already possess will support you to think about what could be transferrable and, indeed, what could be further enhanced as you develop as a social work apprentice.

Bassott (2024) suggests that being self-aware is important to aid critically reflective practice, which, in turn, will aid your learning and development within the workplace. She encourages using a SWOT analysis, which looks at strengths and weaknesses (which are internal) and opportunities and threats (which are external). In order to consider your strengths, ask yourself questions which help to highlight your strengths, abilities and achievements. To consider your weaknesses or, better termed as, areas for development, you may wish to ask yourself questions which highlight what you perceive to be your weaknesses, dislikes and tasks which you avoid. To explore opportunities, consider who and what is available for you to learn from and how you can go about accessing this support. Threats can be explored by considering barriers and distractions, which may discourage or demotivate you. Engaging in this analysis will be helpful at the outset of the programme and, indeed, throughout your apprenticeship journey.

Reflective activity 6.1

At the beginning of your apprenticeship journey, before you meet with your workplace mentor and training provider, write a list of your past employed roles, any voluntary experience you have and the skills you feel you have developed in these roles. Think about any previous training courses you have attended and the knowledgebase that you currently have.

Once you have detailed these things, write another list that could be named a 'knowledge and skills wish list' in relation to your desired knowledgebase and skillset that you aim to achieve within the next twelve months. Share this list and review it each time to meet with your mentor and training provider.

By sharing this information, not only will your workplace mentor and training provider have a good idea of what transferable knowledge and skills you have, but they will be aware of your foresight and commitment to your ongoing learning and development.

Different frameworks at play

As you have already identified in other chapters, there are a range of different frameworks at play over the course of your social work learning journey. Naturally, due to the fact you are doing an apprenticeship, the social work apprenticeship standard is threaded through all that you do in the classroom, in progress reviews and in the workplace. In the same way, given that you are studying a professional programme that leads to qualification, Social Work England professional standards (2019) are too threaded through each element of your learning. When we think about workplace learning in particular, in addition to needing to evidence your development against the apprenticeship standard and Social Work England's professional standards, there are other frameworks in which you are likely going to be assessed against.

BASW's (2018) Professional Capabilities Framework (PCF) is a framework that sets out nine common domains of capability for both social work practice and social work learning. The domains are:

1. Professionalism
2. Values and Ethics
3. Diversity and Equality
4. Rights, Justice and Economic Well-being
5. Knowledge
6. Critical Reflection and Analysis
7. Skills and Interventions
8. Contexts and Organizations
9. Professional Leadership

These nine domains are grouped within the three super domains: Purpose, Practice and Impact:

- Purpose includes Values and Ethics; Diversity and Equality; and Rights, Justice and Economic Well-being
- Practice includes Knowledge; Critical Reflection and Analysis; and Skills and Interventions
- Impact includes Professionalism; Contexts and Organizations; and Professional Leadership

(BASW, 2018)

The framework at a learning / unqualified level seeks to support those undertaking social work study to meet the requirements of the social work regulator (Social Work England) and promotes good practice in relation to supporting you as learners to work towards what would be expected of you in practice (BASW, 2024). As Social Work England stipulates that social work learners undertake so many days in practice in order to develop knowledge and skills in the workplace and be assessed against certain criteria, the PCF sets out a number of what are known as 'level descriptors' against which unqualified social workers can be assessed. Those that apply to you as an apprentice learner are:

- Point of entry to training – the domains at this level will have been considered through your application process and will have underpinned interview questions / assessments and, ultimately, the decision made to accept you on to the programme.
- Readiness for practice – due to you being an apprentice who is employed in a role suitable for the social work apprentice, the domains set out in this level descriptor will, too, have been explored upon entry to the programme. It may also be the case that your training provider

assesses this in a more formal way ahead of you completing your first documented placement.

- End of first placement – each of the nine domains are assessed in detail during your first placement, and usually, a Practice Educator would make a decision as to whether you have provided enough evidence of the capabilities set out in order to fulfil each of the domain areas.
- End of last placement – providing you have fulfilled all domains at the end of the first placement descriptor level, you will then again be assessed against each domain but at a higher level. A Practice Educator again would make an informed evidence-based decision as to whether you have fulfilled and met each of the domain areas.

When you qualify as a social worker, the other level descriptors; newly qualified social worker', 'social worker', 'experienced social worker', 'advanced social worker' and 'strategic social worker' – are descriptors in which you can work towards mapping your capabilities against (BASW, 2024). Please visit the BASW website for full details (https://basw.co.uk/training-cpd/professional-capabilities-framework-pcf).

Some employers and training providers may also begin to introduce the Knowledge and Skills Statements (KSS); these are another set of competency-based statements that determine what is expected of qualified social workers in England. Whilst similar in some respects to BASW's PCF in that the statements seek to promote effective practice in the profession, the knowledge and skills statements are specific to the adult and child social worker role, whereas the PCF at qualified social worker role level and above are generic to the social worker role across the sector.

As you can see, there are multiple frameworks and standards for you to think about, work towards and align with during your training and your future social work career. So, how do you navigate and integrate these frameworks to help ensure your practice aligns with such a multitude of expectations? Sadly, there is no easy way to understand all of these frameworks and standards, so you will have to do this the hard way and familiarize yourself with them all. . . . The good news is that because you will be working within and towards the frameworks discussed, you will naturally become familiar with them; it may not appear to feel this way initially though.

Top tip

Develop a personal reference guide. During your time on the apprenticeship, it would be helpful to maintain a live document which seeks to do the following:

- Summarizes the key aspects of each framework.
- Includes practical examples of how you have demonstrated alignment.
- Tracks your progress in meeting these standards.

There are resources, which you will be able to access, to support you in mapping your learning across the different frameworks discussed above. Your training provider and workplace mentor will provide you with guidance throughout the programme so that you can make these crucial connections. BASW (2020) provide a helpful guide for mapping the PCF, KSS and Social Work England Professional Standards by grouping them into the super domains of Practice, Purpose and Impact, which was referenced earlier. Although this does not include the apprenticeship KSBs, it could form a helpful starting point for mapping the ranging standards and frameworks to your practice. Getting into the habit of recording and mapping your learning daily will help you understand how you are meeting professional expectations.

Reflective activity 6.2

Create your own professional standards mapping document; in order to do this, you will need to access the PCF, SWE professional standards, the apprenticeship standard KSBs, and BASW's Code of Ethics. You may wish to complete your mapping document in a template like this:

Domain / standard	Summary or expectations / requirements	Overlap with other frameworks	Examples in practice
PCF Values and Ethics	Uphold ethical principles in practice	SWE Standard 5: act with integrity KSB - B5: adhere to the Social Work England Standards of Conduct, Performance and Ethics.	Balancing fairness and equity whilst making difficult decisions about how to allocate limited time and resources.

Go through each domain or standard, write it in the first column and provide a brief summary in your own words in the second column. Compare the domain / standard you are mapping to other frameworks. For instance:

- Does the SWE professional standards mention similar values or skills?
- Does the Code of Ethics emphasize a related principle?
- Record these overlaps in the third column.
- As you progress, think about practical examples from your work or studies that align with each standard. These can be added to the last column.

Finally reflect on the following:

- Highlight any gaps where you might need further clarity or development.
- Which domains / standards feel most familiar to me, and why?
- Are there any areas I need to focus on during my apprenticeship?
- How can I use this mapping document to guide my learning and professional development?

Different approaches to work-based learning

Before going on to explore some different approaches, it is important to highlight here that your whole apprenticeship consists of work-based learning; you will be spending approximately 80 per cent of your working week for the duration of your apprenticeship engaging in work-based learning. However, in line with the placement requirements set by Social Work England, you will likely be afforded some placement-specific experiences, and these are what will be explored below.

The placement model

The placement model is the most commonly used model within social work training programmes. Within this, model apprentices are required to complete 200 days of practice learning, thirty of which can be allocated to skills and practice development, also known as 'skills days'. All higher education institutions will vary in how they deliver these sessions, with some not opting to at all and, instead, requiring you to complete all 200 days within a social work placement; others may involve your employer in the facilitation of these. Your first placement will usually last for seventy days, and your final placement will last for 100 days. If you are undertaking an undergraduate degree apprenticeship, then your first placement will be in your second year of study and your final placement will take place in your final year of study. However, if undertaking a postgraduate apprenticeship programme then you will likely have a placement within each year of the two-year programme. In line with what Social Work England would expect, those undertaking social work training programmes should be offered a contrasting placement and a placement whereby statutory work is being undertaken within the team.

Final level placements are usually reserved for statutory settings in line with what Social Work England would expect; however, it is important to note that you may experience two statutory placements depending upon the nature of the work of your organization. Both of your placements will also likely take place within your organization; however, sometimes placement swaps do take place whereby organizations offer a swap with one another, affording you, as an apprentice, some very different placement experiences.

Rotational placements

Within this model, apprentices will rotate through different teams, departments or specializations throughout their duration of study. For example, an apprentice may rotate between a variety of children and families social work teams, such as the initial contact and referral team, duty and assessment, child in need, child protection, looked after children and fostering teams. This provides apprentices with broad exposure to a number of aspects of social work and helps them make connections between how these teams work together to safeguard children. This can also help you, as an apprentice, to identify specific areas of interest and specialization to support your future career development. The drawbacks of this model, however, are that frequent moves may feel disorientating, with the additional factor of the time taken to adapt to new settings. This model can be used separately from the placement model, or it can simply complement the placement model, with apprentices simply rotating to a new team at the point of starting their social work placement. Some organizations use this model whilst others don't, so it is important to seek guidance on the placement model used within your own organization.

Other placements

You may be given opportunities which sit outside of formal and structured social work placements. As stated above, your employer may provide you with additional on-the-job training or even off-the-job training opportunities during times when you are not in university. This could result in you spending time with other teams in your organization for short periods of time. Sometimes, these are known as shadowing placements. For a variety of reasons, you may take part in a split placement. This is when you spend time on placement between two different settings within the same placement period. The reasons for this vary but are often due to organizational issues or the needs of the apprentice and / or teams. Although these can diversify your placement experience, they can also be limiting with respect to the depth of engagement and learning gained. Some universities provide simulated or virtual placements, and these are often used to complement in-person experiences. These placements can be conducted through simulations, role-plays or virtual environments. These can offer a safe and controlled learning environment; however, they will inevitability lack the authenticity of work-based learning.

To reiterate the point made earlier, it is encouraged that you speak to your employer to identify which placement model they offer, as it is common for employers and training providers to take different approaches, particularly where the apprenticeship is concerned.

Evidencing your progress on placement

How you evidence your progress during placement will very much depend on what type of placement model your organization and training provider facilitates. If you were to do a structured placement, which is common practice across the country currently, you will likely have a placement portfolio to complete. It is important to recognize here that portfolios across training providers will be very different; however, you can expect some similarities too. Regardless of the portfolio format, you will likely be asked to evidence a learning agreement; a review that often takes place midway through your placement; reflection on your practice; direct observations of practice; feedback from a Practice Educator, professionals and those with lived experience; and a record of supervision. Your Practice Educator will also likely produce a formal report which evidences your progress against a number of frameworks, such as the PCF and the apprenticeship standard.

It is useful to highlight here that the role of a Practice Educator is to assess you during your structured placements. Practice Educators need to be appropriately trained. Practice Educators are usually only involved during placement times, and at any other time during your apprenticeship journey, it will be your workplace mentor and line manager and possibly others in your workplace who will have a role is supporting and assessing your progress.

Will I be involved in determining work-based learning and placement plans?

Your employer will largely be responsible for ensuring your work-based learning is appropriate to your learning needs and that it meets the requirements of the apprenticeship standard. Your employer will consider a number of factors to ensure they are able to continue meeting the needs of the service whilst you are an apprentice and whilst you are on placement. However, your training provider will have some input and will support you and your employer to think about the following when planning work-based or placement related activities:

- What are your learning and development needs and how will these be met in your proposed team?
- What does a contrasting placement experience look like for you?
- If one of your placements is in your usual substantive team, how can you be supported to undertake different tasks so that you have opportunities for new learning?
- What are your interests? Have you been able to share these?

Using supervision and mentoring to further your learning

In your current role, you may already receive supervision from your manager; however, as an apprentice, there is an expectation that in addition to continuing to receive supervision from your manager, you should be offered protected time to engage in sessions with your workplace mentor. Sometimes, your manager and workplace mentor may be the same person, as explored in other chapters, and sometimes, you have a different person for each role, and so establishing the difference between supervision and mentoring sessions should be confirmed early on in your journey.

Like supervision, mentoring sessions should offer you a safe space in which your practice is central to the discussions had. The key difference between the two is that case management should not really be an element of mentoring sessions, as the focus needs to be on your learning and development as an apprentice and, therefore, is not usually a space to talk about how your casework is progressing. Nonetheless, as you are an apprentice learner in the same workplace as you are an employee, you can reap the benefits of having both supervision and mentoring sessions, and both can enhance your critical thinking, support you to reflect and consider how you can develop and enhance your knowledge and skills. Chapter 9 explores the notion of supervision further and encourages you to think about how you can make the most of it.

Reflective activity 6.3

You may find the below table useful in helping you to think about and plan out the opportunities you feel would support you to develop and enhance your knowledge, skills and behaviours (KSBs) and indeed other frameworks too. This could be referred to in supervision.

Gap in learning:	Which opportunities could help meet this learning need?	When will this be achieved by?	Which ksbs does this relate to?

You may wish to photocopy this and use it to inform discussions in your upcoming supervision and mentoring sessions.

The team around you, the apprentice

One of the real strengths of undertaking the social work apprenticeship is the amount of support you will receive from both your training provider and your employer. Research completed by Stone & Worsley (2022) backs this up with 90 per cent of social work apprentices sharing that they felt adequately supported by their training provider and employer during their programme. This is helpful, given the need for social workers to have a range of support throughout their careers to help them cope with the demands of the role (Collins, 2008). Accessing your support network will not only support you to manage your well-being but will also provide a platform where you can learn from others, whether this is through observation, reflection or problem solving.

It is important that you know how to access this support and that these support mechanisms can work effectively together to keep your learning development journey on track. Chapter 2 explores the key people who will support you during your apprenticeship, and Chapter 9 focuses on how you can manage your well-being; you may find it useful to refer back to these two chapters for more information, so you can think about each topic in relation to how your work-based learning is managed.

Chapter summary

This chapter has focused specifically on the work-based element of the apprenticeship and has introduced the different frameworks at play for those undertaking social work training. The chapter has examined different approaches to work-based learning and has looked in detail at the different types of placement models. Whilst it has been noted in the chapter, it is important to re-emphasize the fact that your training provider and employer may work differently to others, and whilst there will certainly be common trends in how your work-based learning is assessed, it is important to familiarize yourself with how you will be assessed and supported. Taking ownership of your own learning is crucial; however, seeking support from those invested in your apprenticeship journey is also key, as collectively you will be able to tailor your work-based learning experiences so that you can stretch yourself and make excellent progress against the apprenticeship standard. This, in turn, will develop your confidence as you approach qualification.

Recommended reading

The social work degree apprenticeship standard. https://www.instituteforapp renticeships.org/apprenticeship-standards/social-worker-integrated-degree -v1-1.

Social Work England's professional standards. https://www.socialworkengland .org.uk/media/1640/1227_socialworkengland_standards_prof_standards _final-aw.pdf.

BASW. (2018). *Professional capabilities framework.* https://new.basw.co.uk/ training-cpd/professional-capabilities-framework-pcf.

BASW. (2020). *Mapping guidance (adults) and (children & families).* https:// basw.co.uk/policy-and-practice/resources/mapping-pcf-kss-and-regulatory -standards-england.

References

Allemang, B., Dimitropoulos, G., Collins, T., Gill, P., Fulton, A., McLaughlin, A., Ayala, J., Blaug, C., Judge-Stasiak, A., & Letkemann, L. (2022). Role plays to enhance readiness for practicum: Perceptions of graduate &

undergraduate social work students. *Journal of Social Work Education,* 58(4), 652–66. https://DOI:10.1080/10437797.2021.1957735.

Bassott, B. (2024). *Applying social work theory.* A journal. Bloomsbury.

BASW. (2018). *Professional capabilities framework.* https://new.basw.co.uk/training-cpd/professional-capabilities-framework-pcf.

BASW. (2020). *Mapping guidance (adults) and (children & families).* https://basw.co.uk/policy-and-practice/resources/mapping-pcf-kss-and-regulatory-standards-england.

BASW. (2024). *About the professional capabilities framework.* https://basw.co.uk/training-cpd/professional-capabilities-framework/about-professional-capabilities-framework-pcf.

Beasley, P., & Taplin, S. (2023). *Practice education in social work: Achieving professional standards* (3rd edn). Critical Publishing.

Beverley, A., & Worsley, A. (2007). *Learning and teaching in social work practice.* Palgrave Macmillan.

Berrett-Abebe, J., Padykula, N., Clark, M., Zenevitch, R., Bjorklund, D., Gentile, M., Ward, K., & Haven, T. (2023). Social work student reflections on training in integrated care: Opportunities for social work educators. *Social Work Education,* 42(4), 531–47. https://DOI:10.1080/02615479.2021.1976137.

Brown, S. (2019). Using assessment and feedback to empower students and enhance their learning. In C. Bryan & K. Clegg (Eds.), *Innovative assessment in higher education: A handbook for practitioners* (2nd edn). Routledge.

Collins, S. (2008). Statutory social workers: Stress, job satisfaction, coping, social support and individual differences. *The British Journal of Social Work,* 38(6), 1173–93. https://doi.org/10.1093/bjsw/bcm047.

Department for Education. (2023). *Apprenticeship off the job training: Policy background and examples to support the 2023 / 2024 apprenticeship funding rules.* Crown copyright.

Domakin, A. (2014). Are we making the most of learning for the practice placement? *Social Work Education,* 33(6), 718–30.

Gov.uk. (2024). *Adult social work apprenticeship fund.* https://www.gov.uk/government/publications/adult-social-work-apprenticeship-fund#:~:text=Local%20authorities%20can%20apply%20for,adult%20social%20care%20across%20England.

Institute for Apprenticeships and Technical Education (IfATE). (2024) *Training.* https://www.instituteforapprenticeships.org/raising-the-standard-best-practice-guidance/training-raising-the-standards/.

IfATE. (2023). *Social worker integrated degree.* https://www.instituteforapprenticeships.org/apprenticeship-standards/social-worker-integrated-degree-v1-1.

McSweeney, F., & Williams, D. (2019). Social care graduates' judgements of their readiness and preparedness for practice. *Social Work Education, 38*(3), 359–76. https://doi.org/10.1080/02615479.2018.1521792.

Race, P. (2019). *The lecturer's tool kit: A practical guide to learning, teaching and assessment.* Taylor & Francis Group. https://ebookcentral.proquest.com/lib/uocuk/detail.action?docID=5905035.

Showell Nicholas, W., & Kerr, J. (2015). *Practice educating social work students.* Open University Press.

Skilton, C. (2011). Involving experts by experience in assessing students' readiness to practise: The value of experiential learning in student reflection and preparation for practice. *Social Work Education, 30*(3), 299–311. https://DOI:10.1080/02615479.2010.482982.

Social Work England. (2019). *Professional standards.* https://www.socialworkengland.org.uk/media/1640/1227_socialworkengland_standards_prof_standards_final-aw.pdf.

Stone, C., & Worsley, A. (2022). 'It's my time now': The experiences of social work degree apprentices. *Social Work Education, 41*(4), 675–90. https://DOI:10.1080/02615479.2021.1873936.

Smith., M., & Shaw, H. (2022). Learning in the workplace. In C. Stone & M. Shannon (Eds.), *The social work degree apprenticeship.* Critical Publishing.

7

Developing as a reflective practitioner

Mechelle Coulton and Cheryl Lovell

Chapter Outline

What is reflective practice, and why is it so important in
social work? 128

Reflective practice and critical reflection 131

The importance of self-awareness in reflection 135

The importance of professional curiosity in reflective practice 136

What does reflection look like for you as a social work
apprentice? 137

How can others support you to reflect? 138

Reflecting using journals or logs 140

Reflecting using a critical incident analysis 142

Barriers to reflection 142

The apprenticeship standard – demonstrating the
standards through reflection 144

Examples of some additional reflective tools you may
wish to try out 145

Chapter summary 149

This chapter will explore the essential skill of reflection. Reflection is a crucial part of social work practice, and from the very beginning of your social work apprenticeship journey, you will be encouraged to engage in reflection.

Reflection will form part of your day-to-day practice and will enable you to think deeply about the meaning and impact of your practice. Reflective social workers are able to tune in to their practice and use reflection as a tool to unpack their learning in practice and identify developmental opportunities; this is essential, as it allows social workers to think about how their practice could be changed or enhanced, and thus, reflection has a positive impact on those you will go on to support in your social work career. This chapter will introduce reflection as a key component to social work and will have particular focus on the different types of reflection and the difference between basic descriptive reflection and enhanced critical reflection. The chapter will refer to several reflection tools and will include activities to support you as apprentice learners to understand the importance of refection and to be able to effectively apply reflection in your practice.

What is reflective practice, and why is it so important in social work?

When considering the answer to this question and what is meant by the term 'reflective practice', it is worth referring to the work of Donald Schön. Schön (1983) was an educationalist, and his research focused on how professionals from a variety of disciplines developed their respective knowledge bases and how they would use this in practice. What he discovered is that 'knowledge base' as a stand-alone concept would rarely, if ever, give practice guidance. Thompson and Thompson (2018) give examples of this in terms of knowledge of the law and how this does not tell members of the legal profession how to practice law. In a similar vein, knowledge of the human body does not give health professionals a set of instructions to treat illness. This was the area of study Schön focused upon largely, and it was the concept of 'reflective practice' that supported him to do this (Schön, 1983).

Mantell and Scragg (2023) state that reflective practice is important across healthcare and allied professions such as nursing, education and also social work. Reflection is applied to relatively complicated situations and circumstances where there is no obvious solution and requires further processing of the knowledge and understanding that we already possess.

Maclean (2010) highlights the importance of reflective practice in social work by emphasizing the following points:

- Reflective practice is a key aspect of professionalism.
- It is linked with the learning we gain from university and work-based learning, therefore enhances professional development.
- Reflective practice improves practitioner accountability in decision-making.
- It promotes better social work practice and improved outcomes for those with lived experience.
- Reflective practice challenges a practitioner to explore the basic assumptions that underpin their work and helps ensure ethical practice.
- There is a link between the skills and qualities required for reflective practice and the skills and qualities required for best practice in social work.

Maclean (2010) argues that the people with lived experience we work with deserve to work with a practitioner who understands the importance of the work they do and who makes the time to reflect upon it. Reflective practice is a critical examination of a social worker's practice in gaining insight, self-awareness and direction. It can help social workers identify areas for improvement, recognize their learning needs and celebrate successes. Reflection can also help social workers develop strategies to cope with stress, such as setting boundaries and seeking support. After a challenging session with an individual who has experienced trauma, social workers should take the time to reflect on their own feelings about the situation to ensure that they are working effectively and objectively with the individual to ensure that personal values and biases are not impacting decision-making. The concept of vicarious trauma should also be considered when working with those who themselves experience trauma; this is explored in more detail in Chapter 9.

When considering 'reflective practice' from your perspective as an apprentice learner, you will need to think about how you integrate theory / knowledge gained through classroom learning within your practice. It is useful to question here whether it is the theory that underpins practice or practice that informs theory. Traditional approaches would begin with theory and then seek to apply it in practice; however, Thompson and Thompson (2018) argues that it is much wiser to begin with practice and then to draw upon our knowledge base as required as a way of understanding the situation and associated behaviours, which then supports the planning and setting of useful actions. Interestingly, Dewey (1933) believed that people only begin to reflect when there is a problem to be solved; because of this, he outlined five steps for reflective thinking in this circumstance:

1. Define the problem.
2. Analyse the problem.
3. Establish criteria for a solution.
4. Generate possible solutions.
5. Choose the best solution.

Reflective thought

Can you think of a problem you have experienced and apply the steps above to support you to consider the possible solutions?

Schön (1983) introduced both reflection in action and reflection on action, and these ideas became very popular within professional training programmes, including social work. Killion and Todnem (1991) added a third stage of 'reflection for action'. Killion and Todnem (1991) argued that Schön had missed a fundamental stage within the reflective practice cycle that could aid impactful practice. Maclean (2023) refers to the stages as a cycle which supports us to understand the stages of reflection more easily. The cycle considers reflection from three key positions:

- Reflection for action (this happens before).
- Reflection in action (this happens during).
- Reflection on action (this occurs afterwards).

Reflection *in* action can be seen as problem solving in the moment and theorizing in practice. It's the evaluation of thoughts during action. Schön (1983) describes this as 'thinking on our feet'. Reflecting in action allows practitioners to act on something almost immediately.

Reflection *for* action describes the planning and preparation for an intervention. This is arguably the most important stage of reflection, which can often get neglected due to shortage of time and high caseloads amongst the practitioners that would see the value in this stage of reflection. Helpful reflective tools to use for reflection *for* action could be the FOR Model (Maclean and Roberts 2023) and the PREPARED Model (Maclean & Roberts, 2021).

Reflection *on* action can be understood as the ideology of looking back on a situation or intervention and allows for longer term reflection, which can influence meaningful action planning. It also provides you with the opportunity to explore other people's views and allow for more in-depth critical analysis. Most reflective models base themselves upon reflection on action. Some examples of reflective tools that support reflection *on* action are Kolb's Reflective Cycle (1984), Gibbs Reflective Cycle (1988) and the Weather Model (Maclean, 2016).

Reflective activity 7.1

Take some time to research the different models identified above. Have a go at trialling some of them, and see which one you feel the most comfortable with.

Sometimes, it can take trying lots of different models to find the one that works best for you. Moreover, some apprentices have found that using a range of different ones for different situations can be helpful too.

Reflective practice and critical reflection

Basic reflection is when we pause to consider a situation and consider what we think about this. Critical reflection is much deeper than this and promotes an enhanced type of thinking whereby we consider our values and potential conscious and unconscious biases that we may have and openly reflect upon whether these may have impacted our decision-making. It is often considered more helpful to have these reflective discussions during supervision with your managers or even within group / peer supervision where others may really challenge your views and encourage you to think even more deeply about the 'why'. A lack of critical reflection can result in poor practice and decision-making. Williams (2021) believed that critical thinking and listening to others is essential if we are to overcome our unconscious bias. Chapter 8 focuses specifically on critical thinking and will support you to think about how you can develop your critical thinking, which, in turn, will authentically support you to develop your reflective thinking skills.

Fook (1996, 2012) believes that reflection encourages an awareness of socio-political contexts and allows us to explore personal biases and values, thus, enabling us to think about how these may impact social work practice.

Critical reflection, however, takes this a step further and involves thinking critically about roles, interactions and positions of power to improve our practice (Fook, 2012,). Thus, critical reflection is a more in-depth process of thinking about the conditions that shape our actions and seeks to examine how we feel about our actions; this, in turn, results in changes to be made which will enhance future practice.

Ford, Jones and Bratt (2022) suggest some important components for critical reflection. Below, these components are summarized in a way which will help you to think about how you can apply them.

- As an apprentice, you will draw upon your experience of using new learning or new theory.
- You will challenge your own assumptions, beliefs, and ideas.
- The reflection you undertake may focus on a particular event or an incident.
- The reflection you undertake will pick up on initial thoughts and insights and allow you the opportunity to analyse these further and gain a deeper insight.
- By engaging in critical reflection, you will begin to ask the question 'why'. Why did this happen and why did someone act this way?
- Following the analysis stage of reflection, you will develop confidence in thinking about the 'what?'. What needs to happen now? What needs to change?

Reflective activity 7.2

This activity will give you an opportunity to develop your critical reflection skills.

Think about a recent experience that occurred in the workplace that made you stop and think (this could have been an interaction with a colleague or other professional, a meeting you attended, an intervention with a person with lived experience).

Consider the following questions and write your responses down:

What?

Describe in less than 100 words what happened?

This is the descriptive part of reflection, the context, the basic overview to set the scene. What was your role? What decisions were made? What was the outcome?

So what?

This is the analysis part of reflection and the part that allows you to move from basic descriptive reflection to critical analytical reflection. Ask yourself the following:

- Why do you think things happened the way they did?
- What do you understand about the situation, about the method of practice you used, your communication style, your values?
- What influenced what happened?
- Is there a theory that is relevant that could explain what happened?
- Did things happen the way you had intended? If not, why not?

Now what?

This part focuses on action planning.
Think about what could have been done differently.
    What were the key learning points for you, and how will you use these to inform your future practice?
    What do you need to do to improve your practice going forwards, and how can you achieve this?
                                    (Rolfe et al.'s (2001) reflective framework)

Fook and Askeland (2006) discuss a questioning approach and consider the notion of not taking things for granted. Critical reflection involves thinking about the conditions that shape our actions and how we feel about our actions. A key aspect of critical reflection is considering our own frames of references (Mezirow, 1998), which includes our assumptions about the world, about the people we work with and about ourselves. Mezirow (1998) also believes that it includes 'cultural codes, social norms, and ideologies' (p.70). When you begin to consider your thoughts and feelings, you will develop your awareness of your values, biases and cultural views that may impact your thinking in practice. Dewey (1933) believed that people should consider their beliefs and knowledge, and that they should use reasoning to develop ideas and test them through action. Laming (2009) believes that supervision is the cornerstone of social work practice and can prevent unsafe practice, in addition to promoting good outcomes for those with lived experience.

In order to be able to critically reflect, critical thinking skills must be established. The concept of critical thinking is explored in depth in Chapter 8.

Reflective activity 7.3

Reflecting upon your values and perceptions

The activity below will encourage you to discuss your value base with others and reflect upon how this could potentially impact your decision-making in practice. Explore beyond your initial reaction to the subject; do your views change depending on the context? For example, do you view those that solely rely on benefits and those that receive benefits as a top up to their income whilst working differently?

Subject	Your parents' view	Your partner / friend's view	Society's prevalent view	Your personal view	How might this influence your thinking?
People on benefits					
Transgender rights					
Immigration					

(Taken from 'Developing together: social work teaching partnership (2015n.)')

It is important that social workers practice in an anti-oppressive manner; this also applies to you as social work apprentices. Firstly, it is important to recognize that oppression exists, and anti-oppressive practice aims to mitigate the effects of oppression and manage power imbalances. To do this, it is wise to reflect upon your own biases, assumptions and power dynamics that can affect your interactions with others. The key principles of anti-oppressive practice are self-reflection, empowering those with lived experience, working in partnership and providing minimal intervention. These ideologies can be linked to working in a strengths-based way, and Thompson's (1997) PCS model is relevant here too.

Reflective thoughts

Consider the following questions:

- How does your identity create positions of privilege?
- How do your privileges impact your ability to meet people's needs?
- Who is accessing your support, and who is not?
- What barriers are preventing people from accessing support from you and the service you work for?
- How can you work collaboratively with people to meet their needs?

The importance of self-awareness in reflection

Goleman (1998) outlines five components of emotional intelligence which are self-regulation, self-awareness, motivation, empathy and social skills. Mantell and Scragg (2023) suggest that it is important to 'recognise the function of our emotions in alerting us to situations that we need to pay particular attention to' (p.43). Cottrell (2017) says that our emotional responses can negatively impact our capacity to think critically, and we need to be aware that certain situations may trigger us. Learning from experience and by experience is argued to be an essential part of social work training (Mantell & Scragg, 2023). Grant and Kinman (2012) believe that emotional intelligence plays an important role in building resilience. Research by Clarke (2006) indicates that emotional intelligence can be enhanced through reflection.

It is widely accepted that burnout in social work is common. Burnout as a term was first applied by Freudenberger (1975) to describe what happens when a practitioner becomes increasingly inoperative. Practitioners can feel fatigued, exhausted and overwhelmed, which can potentially lead to decreased productivity and poor decision-making. Social workers are often exposed to the effects of trauma which can result in compassion fatigue (Newell & MacNeil, 2010). This is why self-care is important, and to practise self-care, self-awareness is crucial. Self-care and well-being management will be explored in detail in Chapter 9, and there are different concepts and activities to work through to further develop your thinking and connect the themes explored within this chapter. As a social work apprentice and in the future as a social worker, you may often feel a sense of guilt for needing to take care of yourselves as you view your role as being to support others. However, if you are not feeling your best self, then how effective will your actions and decisions be?

A useful tool to consider when reflecting upon your own self-awareness is the Johari window introduced by Luft and Ingham (1955); an example of the window has been created below, adapted from Luft and Ingham (1955). This model encourages you to think about how you see yourself, how you think others perceive you, and areas in which you may be unsure of in relation to what others may see in you.

	Known to you / the self	Not known to you or by the self
Known to others (others can see)	OPEN SELF	BLIND SELF
Not known to others (others cannot see)	HIDDEN SELF	UNKNOWN SELF

The importance of professional curiosity in reflective practice

Mantell and Scragg (2023) argue that practitioners will find themselves seeking clarity and certainty where neither exists. This can result in an over-reliance on procedural approaches to provide that certainty and reduce anxiety; however, this in turn can reduce a practitioner's curiosity. Curiosity is often the motivation for reflection. It pushes us to understand ourselves better, as well as our colleagues, those with lived experience and their carers. A professionally curious practitioner will likely be open to new ideas, feel confident in challenging assumptions and seek alternative ways of doing things. In fact, the lack of professional curiosity has been cited in serious case reviews where social workers had failed to uncover the 'real' story beyond the surface understanding. The importance of asking questions within social work practice is fundamental to best practice, and as a social work apprentice, it is essential that you exercise your professional curiosity, as this is one of the skill statements within the apprenticeship standard (S36). The concept of professional curiosity may feel a little daunting at first; however, through your on- and off-the-job training experiences, you will have lots of opportunities to develop this skill.

What does reflection look like for you as a social work apprentice?

If you are new to reflection, it can initially feel quite a daunting concept to begin to be open and honest about your thoughts and feelings, and you may feel like you may be judged by your workplace mentor, manager and colleagues; this may also raise fears of discovering your flaws or reliving past mistakes or unresolved emotions. However, as you become more comfortable in recognizing your own values, reflecting on your experiences can maximize the potential for new learning. The main barrier to reflection, though, may be finding the time. Reflection is multi-faceted, and how you reflect will depend on many things, such as your physical environment, your job role, the support you receive from your workplace mentor, your learning preferences and your values.

Supervision should be a protected space where you can feel safe to engage in reflection. Supervision should be the place where you can reflect upon the work you have been doing with those with lived experience and begin to make links to social work theory, models, legislation and policy. Supervision is also a good place to think about the impact of your classroom learning and how this translates into practice. The concepts of supervision and application of theory to practice are explored in more detail in Chapters 4 and 9. Reflection is a core component of supervision within social work, and there has been a lot of research undertaken to emphasize the benefits of reflecting on practice within the supervision space. Moreover, you will identify other occasions whereby you find the space to reflect; for example, the commute home from the workplace is a common time to reflect silently and think about the events of the day.

How can others support you to reflect?

To follow on from the discussion above, reflection can be done in different ways – on an individual level immediately following an incident / situation, during one-to-one supervision sessions with a manager or as a group. It has become more common for employers to encourage their staff to create huddles, which can create an environment where learning and reflection can take place, bringing together knowledge, values, innovative ideas and discussion and application of social work theories. This space could also be used to challenge assumptions and test hypotheses. As your confidence and understanding develops, reflection will naturally become more detailed and have more depth. You may start to include law and theory and consider learning from your modules studied, thus creating a holistic view of the situation you are reflecting upon.

Grant and Kinman (2014, pg.12), in their guide to supporting social workers' resilience and well-being, explain that there is strong evidence that supervision, provided on a regular basis within a mutually trusting relationship, is an effective source of support for social workers' . To effectively achieve this purpose, 'reflective supervision should create a safe space for emotional thinking and reflection about ethical and practice-related issues, and conditions where practitioners can be nurtured and helped to flourish' (pg. 12). Davys and Beddoe (2021) argue that good quality reflective supervision is essential to support practitioners to develop professionally, to manage uncertainty and change, to cope with emotions and to grow as critically reflective practitioners. The authors describe a model of supervision, which focuses on supervision as being primarily a learning process. This learning process is driven by the supervisee (this is you as the apprentice), and you as the apprentice and your workplace mentor are 'co-explorers' on a journey. 'Solutions which emerge from the supervision process are discovered and owned by the supervisee rather than taught by the supervisor' (p.101).

Having a trusting relationship with your supervisor (this may be your workplace mentor, your manager or both) in the workplace is said to be essential for open and honest reflections to take place (Yip, 2006). Rankine (2019) believes that supervisors should hear their practitioners 'think aloud' about their casework progress so that they are aware of how their practitioners think and their decision-making processes. The social worker apprenticeship Standard encourages the use of supervision and one of the skills statements (S21) states that you should 'use supervision to support and enhance the quality of your practice'. Engagement in supervision is explored in more detail in Chapter 9. It is also important to have a team who understands the importance of critical reflection and encourages it within the workplace. Sometimes, the culture within teams is not conducive to reflective practice, and this can be challenging. However, whilst studying towards your apprenticeship, you will be encouraged at so many different points to reflect, as reflection will support you to make the links between what you are learning and how you are applying it in practice, and so effectively, it could be said that reflection is the cornerstone of achieving what is required of you in your apprenticeship.

Effective workplace mentors can support you to consider your interventions and decision-making critically, rather than just describing situations. They can facilitate discussions that encourage self-evaluation and exploration of future learning needs, which will lead to more independence in your role. As an apprentice, you can start to reflect upon your transferable skills, perhaps from past working roles or from personal experiences, and link these to in-depth discussions about your values and potential biases that could affect your decision-making and relationships with others. Supervision can be used to scaffold learning, integrating knowledge, skills and behaviours as noted in previous paragraphs.

As emphasized earlier, making the links between theory and practice is an important part of supervision, and as an apprentice, you will be encouraged to make these connections in your regular progress reviews that you will have with your workplace mentor and academic tutor. You may start to understand that you may have been using theories to guide your practice, but you did not have a label, so to speak, to this way of working. For example, you may have always tried to encourage individuals to recognize their strengths but did not identify this as being strengths-based practice. This notion is explored further in Chapter 4. Additionally, reflecting upon feedback from colleagues, workplace mentors, managers, academic staff and individuals that you work with is key to developing your practice. Although you may be fearful of requesting feedback and feel somewhat vulnerable, it is important to seek feedback, and this strengthens your future decisions. To make sure that you receive objective and constructive feedback, observations of your practice are a good starting point.

Reflective peer and group support sessions may also encourage and promote learning within the workplace. Group sessions could provide a safe and supportive space for open reflection with colleagues and classroom peers. These could be provided and facilitated by your workplace mentors or your training provider and would benefit from being pre-arranged and on a regular basis. This may be something that is offered to you as an apprentice and is worth exploring. Group reflective sessions could focus on an incident or experience, whereby, as an apprentice, you could share in a safe space what went well and what may not have gone so well. A reflective model or tool could be used to facilitate the session and encourage discussions within the group of alternative knowledge, theory and interventions. Group reflection is a useful method of support, as others can share their own learning experiences from similar situations and what went well for them or, indeed, what didn't. The concluding of group reflection sessions often includes the facilitator bringing together the ideas and learning points for you to consider within your future practice. As a newer apprentice joining a group reflective session, you could benefit from the knowledge, ideas and support of your peers who have been on the apprenticeship for longer. This model promotes cross-fertilization of experiences and ideas.

It is important to note here that evaluation of a situation can be subjective, and whilst what was implemented may have worked well for you, your organization or the person with lived experience, this doesn't mean to say that it would work well for others. Further to this, Mantell and Scragg (2023) believe that reflection is only a useful exercise if there is an action plan to support the process.

Reflecting using journals or logs

Reflective logs and journals are often used as part of the social work apprenticeship to support apprentices to develop reflective practice. The structure and style of these may vary across workplaces and training providers; however, the meaning behind them is the same. Using a reflective log to support your developing reflective skills can be really useful, and using one of the models shared in this chapter can support you to implement this. Reflective logs or journals may begin by being quite descriptive but, in time, develop into more critical and analytical reflections, particularly as you progress through your studies.

Cottrell (2010) suggests some points to consider as part of the written reflective log which you may find helpful. Let's look at them:

1. Write down every aspect of the experience.
2. Keep a diary (daily / weekly).
3. Share your thoughts / ideas with others (managers, peers, workplace mentors).
4. Record all significant information about your learning; examples of this could be:
   - Thoughts and feelings about the situation.
   - Thoughts about your learning style and how this helps you learn.
   - Ideas that come from your studies.
   - How your studies relate to you work experience.
   - Relevance of theory to practice.
   - What have you learned about yourself?
   - How are you learning to manage your emotions?
   - What have you found difficult?
   - Class discussions as well as inspirations.

Cottrell (2010) also highlights that keeping a journal or a log can be challenging, especially when trying to keep up with regular entries as often is required on an apprenticeship programme. It is, however, a useful 'habit' to adopt, as it can support you in recording your off-the-job training. You do need to have good time management skills and be motivated to keep on top of using journals or logs, and if this is something you do adopt, the logs or journals provide good evidence of your progress over the course of the apprenticeship.

Top tip

- When you are reflecting upon your learning and considering the new learning to you, make sure you capture this and add it to your off-the-job training log. Remember that your off-the-job training record needs to reflect new learning – examples of reflection are a great way to evidence new learning.

Reflecting using a critical incident analysis

As part of reflecting upon your work-based learning, you may find it useful to use the idea of 'Critical Incident Analysis'. It is important to point out here that the word 'critical' does not necessarily mean that something critical has happened in practice. The word critical can be viewed as the reflection being a critical component to your learning. The situation you reflect upon may be a positive one but one that impacted and changed the way in which you intend to practise in the future.

Critical incident analysis is fundamentally a reflective piece that encourages you to analyse an incident that you have been involved with as part of your work-based learning. Mantell and Scragg (2023) provide the following example of what this could look like:

- A brief description of the incident that occurred.
- Explore why this incident had an impact upon you and what made it 'critical'.
- Discussions around the theoretical concepts that informed your response and / or intervention.
- Reflection upon what has been learned and how this will shape your practice in the future.
- Whilst not specifically highlighted by Mantell and Scragg (2010), consideration of the social context is also a useful addition to the critical incident analysis process, and this allows you to think more deeply about the roots of the situation.

Barriers to reflection

Williams and Rutter (2024) raise the point that some apprentices can become fearful of reflection, believing that discussions around their practice and knowledge may expose them for not meeting expectations. When reflecting, you might select details or include aspects that depict yourselves more favourably because it avoids negative feelings (Shaw, 2016). Whilst self-reflection is an important element in reflective practice, it can be limited by being one-dimensional and based on selectively biased memories (Yip, 2006). One way to try and counteract this would be for others to observe your practice and provide feedback for future development and growth. This would facilitate reflections that are based closer to reality than potential personal biases (Bolger, 2014).

Your ability to be critically reflective can be hampered by your emotional reactions. It can be uncomfortable to reflect upon traumatic experiences because this can often mean reliving the emotions involved; therefore, meaningful critical reflection is vital. Poor relationships with your workplace mentor or manager or differences between supervisor and supervisee can lead to miscommunication and, therefore, an unhealthy environment for open and honest reflection. Knowles (1970) researched the impact of the physical environment and found that if this is not appropriate in meeting the psychological needs of those in learning, then the learning process can be impaired.

Finally, time constraints and heavy workloads can leave little time for reflection in social work practice. Maclean (2010) discusses the link between reflective practice and uncertainty. Maclean explains that reflection creates more and more questions and does not always provide the answers; this may not sit well within an organization where managers seek confident action. Social workers can often fear uncertainty and avoid reflective practice as a result; however, working with the uncertainty is an important aspect of the social work role and a common occurrence. As a result of considering the possible barriers to effective reflection, you may find it helpful to consider what you need to be able to reflect effectively. The following activity may help you to do that.

Reflective activity 7.4

Think about the following questions and share your responses in your next supervision.

Do you feel fully focused to reflect without being easily distracted?
Does your physical environment support reflection?
Do you set dedicated time aside for reflection?
Are you able to be honest and self-critical?
   Can you accept feedback from others, whether this be negative or positive?
   For those in which you answered with a 'no', take some time to develop an action plan which seeks to identify SMART actions that can support you to be able to respond positively to each of the questions above.

The apprenticeship standard – demonstrating the KSBs through reflection

The social worker apprenticeship standard comprises a set of knowledge, skills and behaviours (KSBs) as explored in previous chapters, which together define the full capability to do the role of a social worker.

Whilst it could be said that most of the KSBs have a reflective focus, some of the KSBs specifically aligned to reflection include:

K16: models of supervision, critical reflection, and self-reflection to enhance / change practice.

S21: use supervision to support and enhance the quality of your practice.

B4: commit to continuous learning within social work with curiosity and critical reflection.

As an apprentice, you will have the opportunity to meet each area of the standard through work-based learning opportunities and classroom learning, both of which will form part of your off-the-job training. You may feel you need support to identify and demonstrate how you have achieved each statement within your practice, and therefore, the support and opportunity to reflect within your mentoring sessions and supervisions can be useful as well as identify areas for further development. You will also be encouraged to evidence your learning and progress through reflection during your progress reviews as discussed earlier on in this chapter. Once qualified as a social worker, there is also a requirement to reflect as part of your continued professional development (CPD). Social Work England standard 4.6 currently stipulates as part of its professional standards that social workers must reflect upon their learning activities and evidence what impact continuing professional development has on the quality of their practice (SWE, 2019, 4.6).

Social Work England also states:

Reflection involves reviewing your experiences to help make positive changes for your future practice. It turns your experiences into learning and helps you improve your practice in a way that is right for you. Critical reflection moves beyond this and encourages you to examine your approach, judgements, decisions, and interventions. It also involves looking at the steps taken to provide objective support, free from your own views and beliefs. Being able to critically reflect on your practice will help you identify your learning needs and create a cycle of experience, reflection, learning and change.

(SWE, 2019, 4.6)

This demonstrates that even beyond your apprenticeship journey, the need for reflection is essential, and so the sooner you develop the confidence in your reflective skills, the easier it will become for your future practice.

Examples of some additional reflective tools you may wish to try out

It is important to recognize that there are many reflective tools / models which you may find useful as a social work apprentice. Some may lend themselves more towards your style of learning and reflection, and some may be useful to a particular learning activity whereas others may not. Personal preference is key here. Below are three examples for you to consider using (these are in addition to those introduced and discussed in this chapter).

Rolfe et al.'s (2001) reflective framework

This is one of the simplest models of reflection yet so effective as it only includes three stages and encourages critical reflection. The model is based on three questions. Driscoll (2007) also introduced a very similar model, which guided practitioners to respond to the three key questions.

What?

This is the descriptive level of reflection.
What was the issue / what happened during the intervention? Describe it.

So what?

Theory and knowledge building.
    What did I learn? What did it teach me? What did it mean for the person I was interacting with? How did I feel? What was the impact? What could have changed?

Now what?

Action orientated (reflexive) reflection.

What do I need to do now? What can I do to improve my practice next
    time? What other issues need considering? How will I achieve this?

The What? Why? How? Framework

This is often used for reflective practice and is a good starting point
for you as an apprentice to explore the following:

- What is happening here?
- Why has this situation occurred?
- How can I support to bring about change in this situation?

Siobhan Maclean (2023) argues that some practitioners can often
lose their 'why' and may instead think in the following way: what has
happened now? How do I deal with this situation? Maclean (2023)
argues that practitioners should always have the 'why' at the heart
of their practice.

Simon Sinek (2011) developed the 'Golden Circle' model which
firstly asks the question 'Why?' followed by 'How?' and 'What?' The
model has been adapted below:

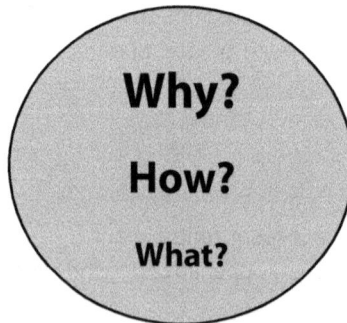

Try using this model to reflect upon a recent challenging situation
you have been involved in. Begin by asking the 'why' question: why
has this situation occurred? How can I support to bring about change
here? What is happening?

The Weather Model (Maclean 2016)

This model introduced by Siobhan Maclean (2016) uses the weather as an analogy for reflective practice and is popular amongst more visual learners. Think about a recent situation you were involved with – this could be within work or your personal life – and consider the following:

Sunshine – What do you feel went well?

What do you feel worked, or what you are particularly proud of? Focus on strengths.

Rain – What do you feel did not go well?

Identify areas for improvement and consider what could have gone better.

Rainbows:

Red (Relationships) – How well were these developed?

Orange (Organization) – What organizational issues impacted our practice?

Yellow (You) - What impact did you have? How have you developed your practice?

Green (Goals) – What were your goals? Were these achieved?

Blue (Barriers) – What barriers did you face? How did you address these?

Indigo (Identity) – What similarities were there in the identities of those involved? Could these issues impact practice?

Violet (Values) – Think about personal, professional, organizational and societal values. Where there any conflicts in values, and how were these managed?

Lightning – Did anything shock you about the situation?

Did anything surprise you? How did you deal with this, and what was the impact?

Thunder – Who's voice / opinion was the loudest?

Whose voice is lost? Is the loudest voice influencing decision-making?

Snow – Can anything be seen differently?

What looks different today and why? What could we be failing to see? Do we need to take a closer look?

Ice – Did anything slip you up?
Have you seen and considered all the risks? Have you planned for these, and what are the dangers?

Fog – What do you feel you couldn't see?
What aspects were missing? What do we need to help guide us through this?

Hail – Was anything painful?
Reflect on your emotions within the situation, important in developing emotional resilience.

Wind – Did anything blow you off course?
Storms – Was there any significant conflict, pressures or change?

You can find out more about this approach to reflection in the following resource:
Maclean, S. (2016) *A new model for social work reflection: whatever the weather.* Kerwin Maclean Associates.

As we come to conclude this chapter, we wanted to share some top tips with you that seek to summarize the key aspects of the chapter.

Top tips

- Try using different reflective models to find one that suits your learning preference best.
- To effectively manage your time, try to use a journal or a log to record your reflections, as some of this can be used to evidence your off-the-job training too.
- Talk to your workplace mentor about reflection, and ask that it forms part of your supervision.
- Take note of when you independently reflect more effectively and develop more space during this time to engage in meaningful reflection.
- Think about what hinders your ability to reflect and write an action plan that will support you to minimize distractions and find the best environment for reflection.

Chapter summary

As you embark upon, or continue, your journey as a social work apprentice, hopefully you have come to understand that you have a wealth of knowledge and skills from previous working and life experiences that can be transferred to your social work apprentice role and, later, social worker role. The apprenticeship provides you with many opportunities to engage in reflection, and in turn, you will see the progress you make with developing your knowledge, skills and behaviours in addition to making connections between classroom learning and workplace practice. This chapter has sought to examine the concept of reflection from different angles and has emphasized the value in critical reflection. The use of models and theories to support your reflection activity will be a key aspect of your learning to enhance your understanding of how these can guide, support and, sometimes, explain your practice. Using different models to support your reflections will encourage deeper and more critical reflection, and you will start to consider different aspects, such as how current world affairs, politics, social justice and your own value base and biases could impact those that you are working with and your capacity to make decisions that are right for them. Considering power imbalances and how managing this by promoting empowerment and co-production will naturally become part of your reflective discussions, and in turn, you will develop confidence in your own ability to dig deep and critically reflect.

Recommended reading

Maclean, S. (2010). *The social work pocket guide to reflective practice*. Kerwin Maclean Associates.

Maclean, S. (2023). *The reflective social worker: A little practical book*. Kerwin Maclean Associates.

Mantel, A., & Scragg, T. (2023). *Reflective practice in social work*. Sage publishing.

References

Bolger, A. (2014). 'The assessment is in the chat': Analysing conversations in community care. *Qualitative Social Work*, *13*(3), 421–35.

Clarke, N. (2006). Developing emotional intelligence through work-based learning. *Human Resource Development International, 9*(4), 447–65.

Clutterbuck, D. (2014). *Everyone needs a mentor* (5th edn). Chartered Institute of Personnel and Development.

Cottrell, S. (2010). *Skills for Success: the personal development planning handbook.* (2nd edn) Basingstoke: Palgrave McMillan.

Cottrell, S. (2017). *Critical thinking skills developing effective analysis and argument* (3rd edn). Palgrave.

Davys, A., & Beddoe, L. (2021). *Best practice in professional supervision: A guide for the helping professions* (2nd edn). Jessica Kingsley Publications.

Developing together social work teaching partnership. (n.d.). *Identifying your value base.* https://www.developingtogetherswtp.org.uk/wp-content/uploads/2020/11/PCF-2_-Tool-1-Identifying-your-Value-Base-Exercise-updated-2-.docx.pdf.

Dewey, J. (1933). *How we think.* D.C Heath.

Driscoll, J. (2017). *Practising clinical supervision: A reflective approach for healthcare professionals* (2nd edn). Baillière Tindall Elsevier.

Driscoll, J.J. (2007). *Supported reflective learning: the essence of clinical supervision?* Chp 2 in Practising Clinical Supervision: A Reflective Approach for Healthcare Professionals (2nd edition, pp. 27–50). London: Bailliere Tindall.

Fook, J. (Ed.). (1996). *The reflective practitioner.* St. Leonards, NSW, Australia: Allen and Unwin.

Fook, J. (2012). *Social work: A critical approach to practice.* London: Sage publishing.

Fook, J., & Askeland, G. A. (2006). The "critical" in critical reflection. In S. White, J. Fook, & F. Gardner (Eds.), *Critical reflection in health and social care* (pp. 40–53). Open University.

Ford, R. Jones, S. & Bratt, S. (2022). *The Social Work Degree Apprenticeship.* St Albans: Critical Publishing.

Freudenberger, H. J. (1975). The staff burn-out syndrome in alternative institutions. *Psychotherapy: Theory, Research & Practice, 12*(1), 73–82.

Grant, L., & Kinman, G. (2012). Enhancing wellbeing in social work students: Building resilience in the next generation. *Social Work Education: The International Journal, 31*(5), 605–21.

Grant, L., & Kinman, G. (2014). *Developing emotional resilience and wellbeing: A practical guide for social workers.* Palgrave Macmillan.

Goleman, D. (1998). *Working with emotional intelligence.* London: Random House.

Killion, J., & Todnem, G. (1991). A Process for Personal Theory Building. *Educational Leadership, 48*, 14–17.

Knowles, M. (1970). *The modern practice of adult education*. New York: Association Press.

Laming, L. (2009). *The protection of children in England: A progress report*. The stationary office.

Luft, J., & Ingham, H. (1955). The Johari window, a graphic model of interpersonal awareness. *Western training laboratory in group development at* University of California.

Maclean, S. (2010). *The social work pocket guide to reflective practice*. Kerwin Maclean Associates.

Maclean, S. (2016). *A new model for social work reflection: Whatever the weather*. Kerwin Maclean Associates.

Maclean, S. (2023). *The reflective social worker: A little practical book*. Kerwin Maclean Associates.

Maclean, S., & Roberts, W. (2023). *Stages of Reflection: A YouTube video*. Available online at https://youtu.be/KOldHp9fwmw.

Mantel, A., & Scragg, T. (2023). *Reflective practice in social work*. Sage publishing.

Mezirow, J. (1998). Transformative learning and social action: A response to Inglis. *Adult Education Quarterly*, 49, 70–72 .

Morrison, T. (2007). Emotional Intelligence, Emotion and Social Work: Context, Characteristics, Complications and Contribution, *The British Journal of Social Work*, 37, 245–63.

Newell, J. M., & MacNeil, G. A. (2010). Professional burnout, vicarious trauma, secondary traumatic stress, and compassion fatigue: A review of theoretical terms, risk factors, and preventive methods for clinicians and researchers. *Best Practices in Mental Health: An International Journal*, 6(2), 57–68.

Rankine, M. (2019). The "thinking aloud" process: A way forward in social work supervision. *Reflective Practice; International and Multidisciplinary Perspectives*, 20(1), 97–110.

Rolfe, G., Freshwater, D., & Jasper, M. (2001). *Critical reflection in nursing and the helping professions: A user's guide*. Palgrave Macmillan.

Schön, D. (1983). *The reflective practitioner: How professionals think in action*. Ashgate.

Shaw. (2016). Self-reflection in reflective practice: A note of caution. *British Journal of Social Work*, 36, 777–88.

Sinek, S. (2011). *Start With Why: How Great Leaders Inspire Everyone to Take Action*. Penguin.

Social Work England (2019) Professional standards. Accessible here: https://www.socialworkengland.org.uk/media/1640/1227_socialworkengland _standards_prof_standards_final-aw.pdf

Stanley, S., & Mettilda, G. (2020). Professional competencies in social work students: Emotional intelligence, reflective ability and empathy – A comparative and longitudinal analysis. *Social Work Education, 40*(7), 827–42.

Stone, C., & Shannon, M. (2022). *The social work degree apprenticeship*. Critical Publishing.

Thompson, N. (1997). *Anti-discriminatory Practice* (2nd edn), Basingstoke: Macmillan.

Thompson, S., & Thompson, N. (2018). *The Critically Reflective Practitioner* (2nd edn) Palgrave.

Williams, J. (2021). Rewiring my racist brain: A life's work. In T. Moore & G. Simango (Eds.), *The anti-racist social worker* (Chap 6, pp. 52–62). Critical Publishing.

Williams, S., & Rutter, L. (2024). *The practice educators handbook*. Sage publishing.

Yip, K. (2006). Self-reflection in reflective practice: A note of caution. *British Journal of Social Work, 36*, 777–88.

8

Critical thinking for social work practice

Mary Gibson

Chapter Outline

What is critical thinking?	154
Terminology	155
Critical reflection – appreciating different perspectives	156
Critical reflection – appreciating the bigger picture (person in context)	159
Critical thinking and systemic practice	160
Thinking critically about assumptions and biases	162
Critical thinking rooted in social work values	164
Critical thinking leads to action	166
Reflexivity - your 'use of self' in practice	168
Developing a critical stance to knowledge	169
Putting it all together and making decisions	171
Making sense of complex information	172
Critical thinking and analysis in assessment	173
Developing legal literacy	174
Thinking critically about risk	174
Chapter summary	178

This chapter will support you as a social work apprentice to develop your critical thinking and analysis skills. As noted in Chapter 1, there is a clear distinction between critical thinking and higher academic grades. On a similar note, the better your analysis is in your assessments, the better quality the assessment will be. Critical thinking and critical analysis skills are required and viewed as essential skills in both academia and in the workplace; as a result of this fact, this chapter will explore what is meant by critical thinking and critical analysis from both an academic and workplace perspective. In doing so, this chapter will guide you on how you could apply critical thinking and analysis principles to both your academic work and within your workplace setting. This chapter will include lots of reflective activities to support you to think about how you can develop and apply critical thinking in different contexts; additionally, the chapter will refer to a range of models which you should find useful when applying them in your practice.

What is critical thinking?

The idea of critical thinking has been around for a long time! Around 2,500 years ago, the thinker and philosopher Socrates was supposed to have declared that 'the unexamined life is not worth living'. He held dialogues with his pupils, asking them probing questions (this is often called the 'Socratic Method') to uncover and examine their beliefs, knowledge, assumptions and actions. In this way, Socrates taught his pupils to consider many perspectives and to grapple with complexity and uncertainty in order to arrive at sound arguments and conclusions; in other words, to think critically.

Glaister (2008: 8) explains that the idea of being 'critical' in your practice is *not* about criticizing (either ourselves or others), being negative or being destructive; rather, it is about having 'open-minded reflective approaches that take account of different perspectives, experiences and assumptions'. During your apprenticeship and when you become a social worker, you will work with people in many complex and changing situations; being a critical practitioner is about your ability and willingness to hold and work with uncertainty, to consider carefully and draw sound knowledge and evidence, and, at the same time, to hold awareness (and also manage ethical tensions) around the very real constraints that may make up the context around your practice (Glaister, 2008). Rutter & Brown (2020: 58) argue that social work practitioners are working with complexity, risk, uncertainty and continual change on an everyday basis, and this requires an overall approach to practice based on the ability and willingness to think critically or to take a 'critical stance'.

Maclean et al. (2018: 178) explain that WHAT-WHY-HOW questions form the basis of social work, but the central WHY question is at the heart of social work practice and critical reflection. The authors explain that when this WHY question is missing, practice tends to become driven by procedures or managerialist principles.

Reflective activity 8.1

In a supervision / mentoring session, consider the WHAT-WHY-HOW questions as you think about a practice situation, paying particular attention to the WHY question.

WHAT is happening for this person?
WHY has this situation come about?
HOW can we work together to bring about more positive outcomes?

Or,

WHAT am I doing?
WHY am I doing it?
HOW is this impacting the situation?

Terminology

There are many words and phrases in the world of social work which are used broadly to describe aspects of this critical approach to social work practice. These include critical reflection, analysis, critical thinking and reflexivity. To illustrate some of the different words and phrases used to capture the critical approach to social work practice, let's first look at the various social work standards and frameworks that you will encounter on your apprenticeship and beyond. You will become very familiar with the apprenticeship standard (IfATE, 2023) – a set of KSBs (knowledge, skills, behaviours) required for the social work profession – and you will be developing your confidence and competence with these throughout your apprenticeship. These KSBs include a requirement to understand and engage in analysis and critical reflection; for example, the skills descriptor S44 asks you to 'critically reflect on / review practice . . .', and you must 'commit to continuous learning within social work, with curiosity and critical reflection' as a social work behaviour. Elements of critical reflection are woven throughout the Social Work England (SWE) professional standards (2019), such as standard 4.2, which requires social workers to use supervision and feedback to critically reflect on and identify learning needs, including how research and evidence informs practice.

You will also come across the British Association of Social Work's Professional Capabilities Framework (PCF) (BASW, 2018). Domain 6 of the PCF instructs the social work learner to 'apply critical reflection and analysis to inform and provide a rationale for professional decision-making'. BASW's PCF framework is linked to BASW's code of ethics (2021: 12), which states that social workers should be 'striving for objectivity and self-awareness in professional practice' and, to do this, 'should reflect and critically evaluate their practice and be aware of their impact on others'. Fook & Gardner (2007) point out that the literature on this topic of 'critical reflection' is vast and complex, covering a range of professions and with many different terms used to mean similar things. Because the term 'critical reflection' is often used in social work literature, we will now explore this term in a social work context.

Critical reflection – appreciating different perspectives

Critical reflection must involve a 'standing back' to gain a different perspective (Fook & Gardner, 2007). Take a moment to look at this picture and ask yourself – what must happen in order for these two people to get a different perspective and perhaps reach an agreement?

(Image created by Mary Gibson)

Reflective activity 8.2

Can you think of a work situation where 'standing back' and considering another perspective might be helpful? Perhaps the perspective of a person you have not heard from yet? What happens if you strive try to 'see' the situation from the perspective of different people involved, including family members and other professionals?

Maclean et al. (2018) proposed a new model for social work, called SHARE. This model is designed to promote deep critical reflection and analysis, and is based around five key aspects of social work which make up the acronym:

S = Seeing
H = Hearing
A = Action
R = Reading
E = Evaluation

The model invites you to ask questions about your practice and the situations you encounter. We will begin by focusing on the first two aspects – Seeing and Hearing. The word 'perspective' is linked to sight and also to hearing. Throughout the book, which explores the SHARE model, Maclean et al. (2018) emphasize the importance of appreciating and valuing the perspectives of a wide range of 'stakeholders' in social work practice, especially the perspectives of the people with lived experience of social work services.

Reflective activity 8.3

Think about a situation in the workplace. Maclean et al. (2018) invite you to ask these sorts of questions about seeing and hearing perspectives:

What is your view of this situation? Does it differ from the view of others?

How could you see things differently?

What might you have lost sight of?

Have you heard fully from all the key stakeholders?

Whose perspective have you not heard from yet?

Whose voice is the most influential? Why?

The central idea in Cree & Davis's (2006) book *Social Work: Voices from the Inside* is the importance of striving to understand and honour the unique stories of the people with whom we work and recognizing that these perspectives are a crucial source of knowledge. Through taking this 'narrative approach', we can recognize and value the expertise of people in matters relating to their own lives. SWE (2019) instructs you to 'value each person as an individual, recognizing their strengths and abilities'. Your apprenticeship KSBs include the following Skill: 'hear the views of people who use services, carers, their families and communities; recognize their expertise; and enable their views to have validity and influence' (IfATE, 2023). The duty to work alongside people in partnership as far as possible, and to listen to and take account of views, wishes, feelings and beliefs, is also enshrined in legislation; for example, the statutory guidance to the Care Act (Department of Health & Social Care, 2024, 1.14) requires local authorities to promote participation as fully as possible and to consider the person's wishes, feelings and beliefs.

Consider for a moment the following quote from a social worker who had a mental health crisis and was placed on section 2 of the Mental Health Act (Maclean et al., 2018: 285):

> For me the most important elements of real assessment were missing; being validated as a human being, being listened to and actually heard, to be made to feel there is hope and someone to take an interest in my individuality.

Reflective thought

How can you ensure you 'see' and 'hear' the people with whom you work so that this is never their experience of assessment?

Critical reflection – appreciating the bigger picture (person in context)

Fook & Gardner (2007, p.17) argue that critical reflection must be based on an appreciation that each person you work with should be understood in the context of their relationships and interactions, the local environment in which they live, as well as the impact of culture and socio-political structures of wider society (including legislation and policy). This appreciation of the person in the context of their social environment is a core feature of social work. BASW's code of ethics (2021: 5) states that 'social work addresses the multiple, complex interactions between human beings, their social situation and their environment', and SWE (2019) requires you to 'value the importance of family and community systems and work in partnership with people to identify and harness the assets of those systems'.

Reflective activity 8.4

You might consider drawing an eco-map, perhaps in a supervision / mentoring session, to help you to visually explore aspects of relationships surrounding a person you are working with. You might also think about drawing an eco-map together with someone, as a collaborative exploration of relationships.

As you draw a circle in the centre of the piece of paper with the person's name, this is a visual way of placing the person at the centre of your thinking. You then think about the relationships surrounding the person and draw lines to depict these. You could have different sorts of lines to depict the quality of the relationship (for example, a dotted line to depict a weak relationship), and you might include arrows to depict the flow of energy in the relationship.

Maclean & Harrison (2015) give a clear example and explanation of an eco-map. You might also explore using a genogram, which is a visual representation of family relationships in a family-tree structure. Burns & Dallos (2023) provide guidance on using a genogram.

Critical thinking and systemic practice

This way of understanding the person embedded in their social context is called having a 'systemic approach' to your practice (Burns & Dallos, 2023), which the authors explain is a collaborative approach 'with the intention of finding a way through complexities and uncertainties'. Using a systemic approach, you are invited to maintain an open-minded attitude, which is often called a not-knowing or non-expert position. Gardner, Fook & White (2006, cited in Thompson & Thompson, 2023: 24) define open-mindedness as 'an attitude of mind which actively welcomes suggestions and relevant information from all sides'; similarly, Rutter & Brown (2020) suggest that having a commitment to an attitude of openness (rather than a defensive attitude) is a crucial aspect of critical thinking, holding an awareness that we don't know it all! Fook & Askeland (2006) describe having a sense of self which is accepting and comfortable with the realization that other people have other views and perspectives which may conflict with yours.

Alongside, and complementing this idea, you are invited to strive to maintain a curious approach to situations you encounter. Ruch (2018) explains that the concept of curiosity is a central idea in systemic practice (which, in turn, is a key element of relationship-based practice); a curious practitioner explores the sources of strength and resilience in a person's life, takes into consideration multiple perspectives and continues to be curious about the challenges and pressure points without jumping to conclusions. Furthermore, as a curious practitioner, you are willing and able to tolerate uncertainty as you hold many possibilities and perspectives in mind, as well as being open to the possibility of unearthing additional aspects of the situation. Therefore, a systemic approach acknowledges the complexity of people's lives and tries to avoid quick and simplistic responses which fail to look beyond the individual.

The importance of professional curiosity is a theme running through Serious Case Reviews in children's services (Burton & Revell, 2018) and also Safeguarding Adult Reviews (Thacker et al., 2019), and a lack of professional curiosity is identified as a factor in serious incidents. Burton & Revell (2018) argue that social work practitioners need to be supported by the organization to maintain professional curiosity; this involves 'stepping out of the comfort zone' to explore beyond the limits of knowledge and experience and to work with feelings of discomfort, tension and anxiety in uncertain and complex situations in order to come to a transformative understanding of a child's situation. Thacker et al. (2019: 257–8) discuss three overarching themes which are barriers to professional curiosity – the particular 'dynamics' of each case situation, 'professional issues' and 'organizational issues'. Professional issues include struggling with confidence when dealing with uncertainty and tension; holding an attitude where behaviour was seen uncritically as 'normal' (and was not understood within the context of the person's situation); and having 'professional deference' to the opinions of other professionals who were perceived as having higher status. The three overarching barriers to professional curiosity discussed by Thacker et al. (2019) are, of course, inter-related and the authors cite Lyn Romeo (who at the time was Chief Social Worker for England) to highlight the important role of critically reflective supervision in the development of good practice and professional confidence.

Reflective thoughts

To what extent do you feel supported by your organization as you develop your confidence and competence in complex situations? What is positive? Is there anything that might be improved? What support do you need?

Lewis et al. (2022, p.5) argue that social work practitioners should be supported to maintain professional curiosity through the use of 'hypothesising' where practitioners come together to discuss and explore multiple perspectives about what might be happening in a given situation, test assumptions, and ensure that plans are informed by evidence and robust holistic analysis.

Reflective thoughts

Do you have opportunities in the workplace to hypothesize about complex situations? What do you bring to these, what do you learn?

Thinking critically about assumptions and biases

A key element in critical reflection involves the 'unsettling' or 'shaking up' of assumptions (Fook & Gardner, 2007: 67). Fook & Gardner (2007) invite you to imagine a packet of muesli, containing different ingredients, some bigger and some smaller, and different weights. They use this metaphor of shaking up a packet of muesli to illustrate the shaking of assumptions, ideas, beliefs (maybe about yourself, your practice or a particular situation in practice and how you understand this) that were deep down and hidden from awareness. The authors explain that the process of critical reflection shakes these up so that they can be seen, accessed and discussed, and that this process can be unsettling and uncomfortable.

Critical reflection has an important role in unearthing and questioning deep-seated assumptions embedded in cultural norms; in other words the 'thinking and behaviour which is taken-for-granted' yet which often is shared by and defines the culture shared by a group (Fook & Askeland, 2007, p.2). The authors explain that culture may refer to a large group such as a whole nation or society, right down to a small group such as family, community, workplace and friends. And of course, it is important to unearth and examine how assumptions and ideologies live within each one of us and shape our thinking and behaviour. Brookfield (2009) comments that these deep-seated assumptions can be hard to uncover as they can be embedded in education, in the media, politics and institutions of society – in other words hiding 'in plain sight'. This way of thinking is what Rutter & Brown (2020:

5–6) describe as having 'a certain amount of professional scepticism, i.e. when nothing is regarded as a universal truth, or taken on trust anymore'.

Reflective activity 8.5

In a supervision / mentoring session, you could bring a practice situation and reflect on this with a focus on examining any assumptions which could have been made (for example this could be something you have read in case notes or in a referral).

You might think about how the norms and values held by this society might be influencing the lived experience of someone you are working with and what might be influencing your own thinking and beliefs. You could think about how the culture and processes of the organization in which you work could influence the way you approach the situation?

Critical thinking must involve having curiosity about our own and others' natural human tendency to take short cuts in our thinking, which can lead to bias or prejudging a person or situation. In particular, we tend to give more value to viewpoints which are closer to our own and to place less emphasis on conflicting viewpoints (Rutter & Brown, 2020). These biases need to be uncovered and explored. Rutter & Brown (2020: 7–8) offer a list of examples of bias in thinking and behaviour, including the following:

- Anchoring effect – tendency to rely too heavily or 'anchor' on one trait or piece of information when making decisions.
- Bandwagon effect – the tendency to do or believe things because others do (for example a biased team perspective of the situation)
- Confirmation bias – tendency to search or interpret or take notice of information in a way that confirms what you want to believe.

In addition, Munro (2020, p.50) explains that 'hindsight bias' is a distortion in thinking where we tend to judge a situation by its outcome. Munro notes that this is well-known in child protection, where an outcome appears obvious when viewed through the lens of hindsight; in other words, the tendency is to overestimate what could or should have been anticipated. Another error in thinking raised by Munro (2020: 49) is 'fundamental attribution error', which is our tendency to judge someone's behaviour as the result of characteristics internal to the person rather than any external factors. In their list of biases, Killick & Taylor (2024: 105) include 'prejudice', which is an evaluation of a person that arises from conscious or unconscious stereotyping (the tendency to make assumptions about people based on general characteristics presumed to be associated with a group of people).

Reflective thought

Can you think of any workplace situations where one or more of the above biases might have been happening?

Critical thinking rooted in social work values

Any discussion about critical thinking must recognize and be firmly rooted in the value base which is fundamental to social work practice, which includes respecting others as equals and striving for empowerment and anti-oppressive practice (Glaister, 2008). Imagine for a moment a mature tree standing tall, full of healthy leaves. You may have a particular tree in mind, perhaps in a woodland or in a field or in a local park. Think about the strong roots which, although hidden below ground, continually nourish the tree and support it to stand firm through all weathers. Now, imagine that the roots are your social work values, which nourish, strengthen and renew your practice and which help you to stand firm in the many workplace situations you do and will encounter. Your social work behaviours and skills are the healthy visible 'branches' and 'leaves' of your practice that people see as you go about your job role; and these rely on your strong and stable value roots.

BASW's code of ethics (2021: 4) states that 'respect for human rights and a commitment to promoting social justice are at the core of social work practice throughout the world'. The apprenticeship KSBs require you to develop your understanding of 'the impact of injustice, demography, social inequality, policies and other issues which affect the demand for social work services', and Social Work England (2019) states that social workers must 'recognise differences across diverse communities and challenge the impact of disadvantage and discrimination on people and their families and communities'.

Social work practitioners must develop an appreciation that people (including ourselves!) live complex lives and have diverse identities, all of which intersect in unique ways (Tedam, 2024). A nuanced understanding of a person's lived experience, including that of oppression, can be developed using the 'lens of intersectionality', defined by Tedam (2024: 12) as 'the way in which the interconnections of social categories such as race, gender, age, ability and class create unique experiences of discrimination and oppression'; conversely, aspects of identity can confer power and status. Bernard (2022: 25) comments that intersectionality is a tool rooted in anti-oppressive principles, which can help to promote your critical engagement with those intersecting systems of oppression such as disablism, racism, sexism and heterosexism. This should include developing your awareness of your own intersecting aspects of identity, what these mean to you and how they affect you – what Bernard describes as 'your own positionality'.

To help you to explore intersectionality further, you might consider using the Social Graces (GRRAAACCEEESS) model (Tedam, 2024). This was originally described by Burnham (2012) as a tool to help practitioners to be aware of and attend to personal and social aspects of identity, whether these are visible or invisible, voiced or unvoiced. The Graces are an acronym to represent many aspects of identity, as you can see in Reflective activity 8.6.

Reflective activity 8.6

You might think about these words in the list below and consider these aspects of your own identity. Is this an important aspect of your own identity? Do you think you are in a relatively privileged position for this identity? You might then look at this list thinking about aspects of identity for a person you are working with. You might consider using this model as a way of exploring this topic in a collaborative way alongside someone.

Gender identity	Appearance	Economics (finance)
Geography	Accent (or language)	Education
Race	Class (and housing)	Sexuality and sexual orientation
Religion	Culture	Spirituality
Age	Ethnicity	Any others you can think of!
Ability (disability)	Employment	

Therefore, critical reflection in social work must involve an understanding of the impact of power and powerlessness in the lives of the people you encounter in order to act in an anti-oppressive way (Maclean et al. 2018). Brookfield (2009, p.297) argues that reflective practice only becomes 'critical' when the spotlight is sharply focused onto 'issues of power and control' in order to uncover and also challenge the power dynamics and wider structures that impact and surround the people with whom you work. This, of course, includes your own critical awareness of the power dynamics that permeate your professional practice. Maclean et al. (2018: 270) pose some questions which might help you to critically reflect on power dynamics:

- *Where* does power lie in this situation?
- *How* is power being used? How does the experience of powerlessness impact?
- *Why* is the power dynamic like this?
- *What* aspects of my practice are empowering? *What* aspects of my practice are disempowering?

Critical thinking leads to action

Returning to the SHARE model (Maclean et al., 2018: 177), the A of SHARE stands for Action. The authors state that A is the central letter, and 'Action' is central to the SHARE model and to social work practice. Your actions are how you demonstrate in practice that you are rooted in and nourished by your social work values, which are displayed in your social work skills and behaviours in every encounter.

Fook & Gardner (2007: 16) emphasize that critical reflection 'links changed awareness with changed action'; in other words, your critical thinking should result in action. Thompson & Thompson (2023: 28) argue that a critical understanding of a person's situation, which includes critical depth (looking beneath the surface of the situation, for example, scrutinizing assumptions) as well as breadth (understanding the situation in the context of the wider social and political picture), must lead to a transformed perspective which is emancipatory in approach – 'that is, one that helps to free people up from the restrictive aspects of their social circumstances (e.g. discrimination, stigma, poverty and so on)'.

A culturagram is a tool which can help you to understand and be sensitive to a person's cultural and ethnic background. Parker (2025) explains that using this tool aims to position the person as the expert of their own lived experience, and its use requires excellent communication skills as you collaborate to explore the topics in the box below:

Time in the community	**Family Members**	Age of family members at the time of immigration
Language spoken at home and in community		Contact with cultural institutions
Reasons for immigration		Health beliefs
Legal status		Impact of crisis events
Holidays and special events		Family, education and work values

Adapted from Parker's culturagram (2025, p. 82)

To help you to focus on action and to actively engage in anti-oppressive practice, it might be helpful to consider Tedam's (2024: 52–4) 4D2P framework. The four Ds stand for the following:

Discuss: open up a safe space for collaborative discussion as far as you can. Be mindful of language / jargon, and use active listening skills to explore and understand the person's situation.

Discover: be open to discovering more about yourself and the other person as you explore the situation collaboratively. Try to uncover any areas of oppression the person might be experiencing. You might use the Social Graces model described earlier, or a culturagram, to help your exploration at this stage.

Decide: at this stage, you are moving towards deciding on the best course of action. This must involve taking full account of the voice / perspective of the person you are working with (and may involve collaborating with others) to promote and offer choice as far as possible.

Disrupt: this involves acting as far as you can to counter any oppression the person may be experiencing and, at the least, ensuring that this is not promoted or maintained. Tedam (2024: 53) states that 'the aim is to disrupt oppression and oppressive systems'.

Throughout all of the above four Ds, you must be continually aware of two Ps – *Power and Privilege* – and how these might be influencing your practice and how these might be impacting you and the person you are working with.

Reflexivity - your 'use of self' in practice

Parker (2025) notes that a reflexive approach is central to action. Reflexivity is defined as 'the ability to recognize our own influence – and the influence of our social and cultural contexts . . . it is about factoring ourselves as players into the situations we practice in' (Fook & Askeland, 2006: 45). This ability to 'see' yourself in practice must be developed on an ongoing basis throughout your apprenticeship and in your social work career (for example see SWE standard 4) as you critically reflect on your thoughts, feelings and actions in practice situations. Schön (1983) argued that professionals should reflect-in-action and on-action. The former is a quality of checking in with yourself during a social work encounter to reflect on your own thoughts, feelings and beliefs; the knowledge you are using; and your behaviour in order to make adjustments. You supplement this with reflecting-on-action – looking back on the encounter and learning from the experience. This might happen in a supervision / mentoring session where you are supported to ask questions such as 'how did that go?', 'how was the person feeling?', 'how do I feel now?' and 'what might I have done differently?' Killion & Todnem (1991) developed Schön's stages of reflection to include reflecting-for-action, explaining that the three stages of reflection together encompass the past, present and future. Reflecting-for-action could involve checking in with yourself prior to an encounter, as well as being aware of your feelings and the knowledge that might be influencing you. In relationship-based social work, your professional 'use of self' is fundamental to encounters – your main 'tool' is you (Ward, 2018).

Reflective activity 8.7

Imagine you are with someone in a work situation, you put to one side your notebook, assessment tool, pen, tablet etc., and your only 'tool' is yourself. How would you feel?

We are all complex people with many different aspects of our 'selves' (Ward, 2018). To explore aspects of yourself in a supervision / mentoring session, you might use the Johari window (Luft & Ingham, 1955) as explored in Chapter 7. The name is a combination of the original authors' surnames. This model has four quadrants as you can see below:

	Known to yourself	Unknown to yourself
Known by others	Open area (things known to you and to others)	Blind area (things about you that are noticed by others but you are not yet aware of)
Unknown to others	Hidden area (things that are known to you, but not revealed to others)	Unknown area (things not known to you or to others)

Adapted from Luft & Ingham (1955)

As you develop your social work KSBs during your apprenticeship, you will be learning more about yourself as well as about the social work profession. As you receive feedback (for example during supervision and when you are observed in practice), you may discover things about yourself and your practice that you were not previously aware of (your Blind area). You may also discover qualities and strengths in yourself which were previously Unknown to you and others. During your apprenticeship you will be invited to reflect on aspects of yourself that were previously Hidden, bringing these more into the Open area. As you develop your self-awareness, the four quadrants will not always be equal in size.

Developing a critical stance to knowledge

The next letter of Maclean et al.'s (2018, p.217) SHARE is R for 'reading'. This focuses on the knowledge you use in your work.

A range of knowledge should be integrated into your practice in an ever-evolving way so that theory and practice are integrated – 'theory underpins practice and practice informs theory' (Thompson & Thompson, 2023: 20). However, Collingwood et al. (2008) recognized that applying theory to practice can often be challenging for social work learners. In response, the authors proposed a practical theory framework which begins with the person you are working with placed visually at the centre of a piece of paper, with an invitation to explore likes and dislikes, strengths, hopes, priorities, the things that are important to the person and the influence of relationships and the environment around the person. In this way, your starting point and the central component of this framework is your knowledge and appreciation of the person's lived experience. The authors then invite you to consider what knowledge might help to inform your understanding of the person in their situation (for example, theories such as attachment theory, grief and loss theories, poverty, stigma and any relevant research) and, flowing from this (and linking with the person's goals, priorities explored above), what methods or approaches might be appropriate for your intervention with the person (such as strength-based approach). You should also incorporate other knowledge which may be relevant, such as legislation and policy, organizational policies and knowledge of organizational and local resources and their limitations. Throughout the exploration, you ensure your work is rooted in your social work values.

Having a critical stance towards knowledge is essential to effective social work practice (Thompson & Thompson, 2023). Thompson & Thompson (2023: 22) argue that knowledge should be used in an 'open' way; this involves being explicitly aware of the knowledge that is being chosen and used and why you think it is appropriate, being aware that knowledge can be challenged and scrutinized (so that flaws are unearthed and knowledge can be updated) and ensuring that the way knowledge is used aligns with social work values.

Your choice of theory could influence how you understand a person's situation and the actions you might take. It may be helpful to start by thinking about a person you are currently (or have recently been) working with. Choose a theory that could inform your understanding and think about how much you know about it? Are you aware of any recent developments / research? What might be the critiques or limitations of the theory? What might you do to update your knowledge? How might this theory inform your understanding of the person?

Top tips

- Go back to Chapter 4 to support you to think about the above discussion points on application of theory. Use some of the reflective exercises and source ideas shared in Chapter 4.
- Think about what academic study skills you may need to further develop your critical thinking. Ask your training provider what support is available; as discussed in other chapters, your training provider will have specific resources, people and services that can help you to develop your study skills – in particular, your critical thinking – which you can then apply to your assignments.

The truth is that social work practitioners spend a lot of time reading about people and their circumstances, usually in electronic records or case files, often in preparation for an assessment (Maclean et al., 2018: 222). The available information might include previous referrals and assessments, case records and so on. Maclean et al. (2018) comment that reading this information could lead to prejudging a situation, and a balance must be struck between this possibility and the need to be prepared. As a critically reflective practitioner, you will be mindful that the information you read may include a worker's particular opinions and biases or may be influenced by factors such as organizational culture, time-pressures and resource limitations (Parker, 2025).

Reflective activity 8.8

Read this quote from Rosie, who speaks about her experience, as an adult, reading her children's social care records:

> I found it very upsetting some of the time because what you see is how people perceived you and how people came to con-clusions about you, made assumptions and judgments about you without really knowing you . . .

(source: 'Rosie: Accessing my care records' in Shepherd, E. (2022))

As you write records, think carefully about how others will read and interpret the words you have written and what your words will tell them about the person you have written about? What would the person say?

Putting it all together and making decisions

The last letter of the SHARE model is E for evaluation (Maclean et al., 2018: 255). The authors explain that evaluation is about turning knowledge into understanding; it is about putting together everything you have seen, heard, done and read and being able to explain WHY you have arrived at a certain conclusion.

Making sense of complex information

The tool below is called Wonnacott's Discrepancy Matrix. This tool encourages you to examine and critique information relating to a case situation with the overall aim of developing your confidence working with complex information where there are elements of uncertainty (Earle et al., 2017).

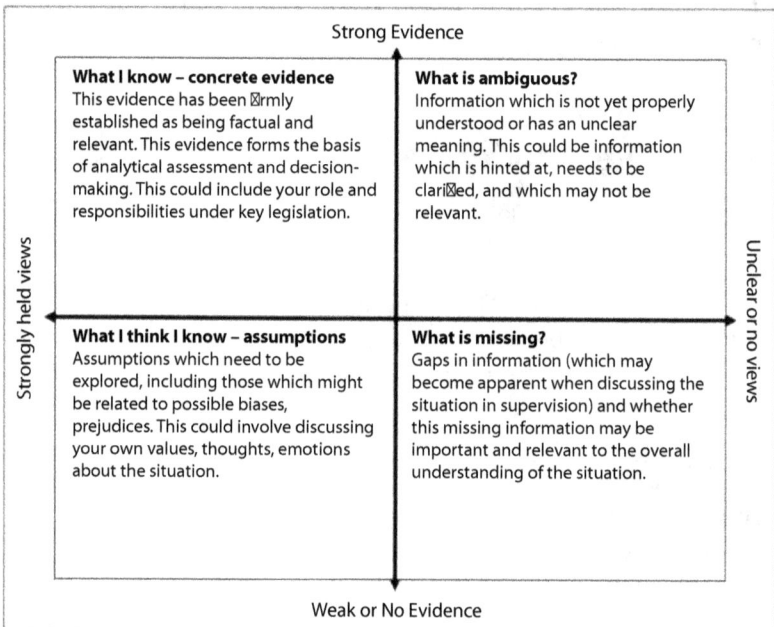

Adapted from Morrison & Wonnacott (2009) in Wonnacott (2014: 87); Earle et al. (2017: 74–5).

Reflective activity 8.9

Think about a person or family you have recently started working with. Sort the information you have received or gathered into the four types shown above: evidence, ambiguous, assumption and missing. With your supervisor / mentor, discuss your findings for each of the four areas and agree what you need to do next.

Critical thinking and analysis in assessment

The importance of critical thinking and analysis in assessments is well-established (Munro, 2011; Turney, 2014). Writing an analytical assessment involves sorting through complex and often confusing or incomplete information, determining how much weight and validity to give to different themes and factors, and being able to clearly evidence your reasoning so you can demonstrate how you arrived at your professional judgements (Brown et al., 2014). Effective social work practitioners also develop intuitive reasoning skills through critically reflecting on work experiences (Munro, 2011). Intuition (being aware of a hunch or gut feeling), when used cautiously and with open-minded awareness, is an important aspect of thinking in complex situations (Brown et al., 2014).

Brown et al. (2014) suggest that an analytical assessment should include the following qualities:

- Gives a clear objective picture of the child / family / person you are assessing.
- Information is specific throughout (avoiding vague and general statements).
- Is concise, relevant and free of jargon.
- Is logical – your thinking process is clear for the reader to follow (show your workings out!), and it is evident how you reached your conclusions / recommendations.
- Makes use of relevant underpinning knowledge and evidence to support your analysis.
- As a result of the above, your conclusions about likelihood and seriousness of harm are clear and evidence informed. This is often called defensible decision-making (Domakin, 2022).

Reflective thought

Think about an assessment you have recently completed as you look at the above list. What do you think your strengths and areas for development are?

Developing legal literacy

In order to make decisions which are ethically and legally defensible (to be able to explain and justify how and why the state is intervening in people's lives), social work practitioners need to possess legal literacy (Preston-Shoot, 2019). This is crucial to effective practice and combines three concepts (Braye & Preston-Shoot, 2021; Braye & Preston-Shoot, 2016):

- A detailed and specific knowledge of relevant law and policy, and the ability to apply this to practice situations – *doing right things*.
- A sound awareness of the ethical dimensions of the law in practice situations (for example, balancing the right to autonomy and the right to be protected form harm) – *doing things right*.
- A critical understanding in the use of law and policy in promoting human rights and social justice – *being rights-based*.

Tedam (2024, p.12) points out that if you do not know what a person's rights / entitlements are under legislation, you could be placing restrictions on that person's rights, and this amounts to oppressive practice.

Reflective thought

Think about a work situation involving an aspect of the law. How confident do you feel about putting the above three points into practice? What might you do to build your confidence?

Thinking critically about risk

The assessment of risk is an every-day aspect of social work practice (Parkes, 2023). We are all aware that taking risks, large or small, is part and parcel of being human, and you will no doubt be able to think about risks you have taken (crossing a busy road, for example). Killick & Taylor (2024) explain that a risk is a situation where an outcome is unknown but could be desirable or undesirable. A risk assessment 'tries to understand how likely the harm is and how severe the outcome might be', and the management of risk involves the balancing of benefits and harms (Killick & Taylor, 2024: 7). Munro (2020: 105) points out that child protection work has always involved working with situations where there is uncertainty, and in recent years, the 'problem of managing uncertainty' has been increasingly expressed in the language of 'risk'.

As the diagram below illustrates, the combination of likelihood of harm and severity of the possible outcome gives a rough indication of overall risk (Parkes, 2023). It is important to bear in mind that each situation will be unique and that this diagram is just a starting point to your analysis.

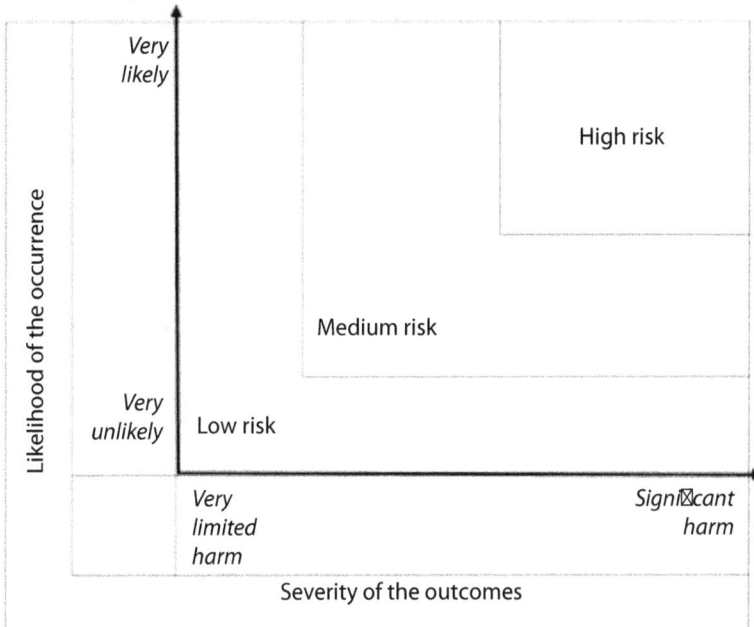

Adapted from Parkes (2023, p.244).

Reflective activity 8.10

Familiarize yourself with your local 'Continuum of Need' criteria in the context of safeguarding children, and find out more about the different thresholds for the state intervening in the lives of children and families.

Munro (2020), writing about child protection, cautions against one-sided assessments which focus solely on risks or deficits and emphasizes the importance of a balanced approach which also considers the benefits of possible options as well as areas of strength and resilience in children, families and communities. The identification of protective factors – those qualities, strengths and resources available to a person or family which can protect against a risk – is an important aspect of a balanced risk assessment (Parkes, 2023). The statutory guidance to the Children Act 1989 (Department for Education, 2023) is clear that assessment must be child-centred and responsive to the child's voice and should holistically consider a range of factors across three domains: the child's developmental needs, the capacity of carers to respond to those needs and the influence of any environmental and family factors. In the assessment of risk in work with children and families, Munro (2020) suggests the following questions:

1. What is or has been happening?
2. What might happen?
3. How likely are these outcomes?
4. How undesirable are they?
5. The overall judgement of risk – a combination of the likelihood and the seriousness

It may be helpful to think about a safeguarding situation you have experienced at work and to consider how might these questions help you in your analysis.

In the context of working with adults, Sanderson & Lewis (2012: 214) describe risk management as finding the 'holy grail' of balancing of 'positive risk taking' and 'minimising harm'. This 'holy grail' has seven criteria (Bates & Silberman, 2007; Sanderson & Lewis, 2012):

1. Involvement of the person and other key people (such as relatives, friends) in risk assessment. This is fundamental to a person-centred approach, which revolves around an understanding and consideration of the wishes, feelings and beliefs of the person; their perspective of the risk; and what they would like to happen.
2. Positive and informed risk taking. This stage involves an appreciation of possible benefits of risk-taking and an understanding of the factors that are *important to* the person (what makes them happy) as well as the factors which are *important for* them (what makes them safer). This will involve application of key legislation, including the Human Rights Act 1998. The following diagram illustrates how a consideration of factors *important to* and *important for* the person should inform decision-making.
3. Proportionality. This legal principle requires you to strike the right balance of rights and risks (Parkes, 2023: 252) as you consider the consequences of taking the risk and also of *not* taking the risk (Sanderson & Lewis, 2012). Read and reflect on the following

statement made by Lord Justice Munby (Local Authority X v MM & Anor (No.1) (2007) EWHC 2003 (Fam)):

> The emphasis must be on sensible risk appraisal, not striving to avoid all risk, whatever the price, but instead seeking a proper balance and being willing to tolerate manageable or acceptable risks as the price appropriately to be paid in order to achieve some other good – in particular to achieve the vital good of the elderly or vulnerable person's happiness. What good is it making someone safer if it merely makes them miserable?

4. Contextualizing behaviour. This asks you to be curious about the reasons WHY the person might have behaved in this way, at this time, in this situation? How likely is this to happen again?
5. Defensible decision-making. This stage requires you to make an 'explicit and justifiable rationale for the risk management decisions' (Bates & Silberman, 2007: 7).
6. A learning culture. This recognizes the importance of the organizational culture in supporting you to develop your person-centred approach to risk.
7. Tolerable risks. This stage recognizes the importance of using creativity on an ongoing basis to continue exploring how to achieve the 'holy grail' of risk management for that person.

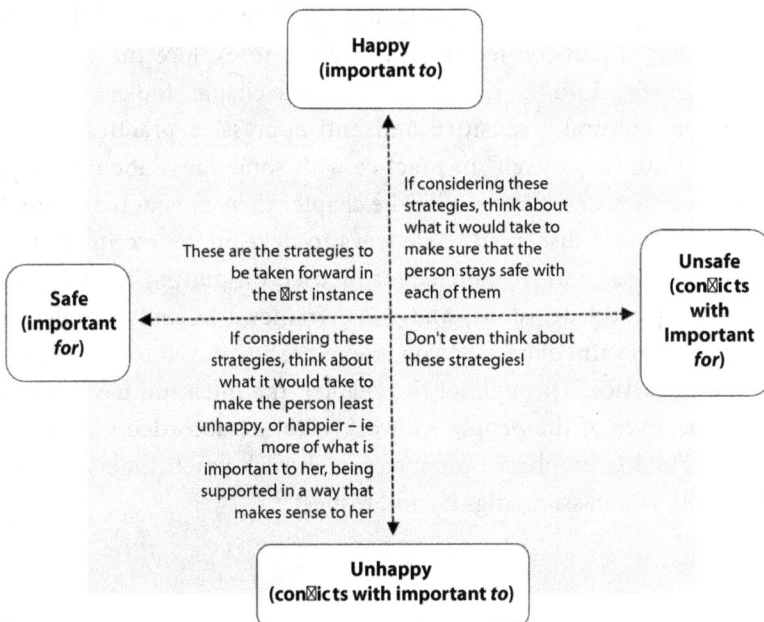

Adapted from Sanderson & Lewis (2012: 218)

Reflective activity 8.11

Try using the above criteria and the safe / happy grid help you to explore and understand an adult's situation where there are concerns about risk. Discuss your learning with your supervisor / workplace mentor.

Chapter summary

This chapter has explored a range of ideas related to critical thinking for social work practice. It started with an overview of critical thinking and the terminology associated with this in the world of social work. Throughout, Maclean et al.'s (2018) SHARE model was used to provide stages on your journey through aspects of critical thinking. We considered the importance of considering the person-in-environment and how systemic ideas and practice, such as developing professional curiosity, are integral to critical thinking. The chapter then focused on some assumptions and biases that we can be prone to in order to 'unearth' and 'unsettle' these and bring them into the open to be examined. The metaphor of a tree was used to make the crucial point that critical thinking must always be firmly rooted in and nourished by social work values, and the following discussion led to an invitation to explore the concept of intersectionality. Into the realm of Action, the chapter looked at models to promote culturally sensitive and anti-oppressive practice, and we discussed your 'use of self' in practice with some ideas about how you might develop your reflexive self. The chapter then considered the realm of knowledge and discussed some ways to develop your critical stance to this. The final part of the chapter focused on putting it all together and making good decisions, and some frameworks and models were offered with the aim of helping you to explore and develop these skills in your own practice. Throughout the chapter, the intention has been that the perspectives of the people we work with are accorded validity and influence, and to emphasize that, as social work practitioners, we treat people with compassion, dignity and respect.

Recommended reading

James, E., Mitchell, R., Morgan, H., Harvey, M., & Burgess, I. (2020). *Social work, cats and rocket science: Stories of making a difference in social work with adults.* Jessica Kingsley Publishers.

Lishman, J., Bolger, J., Gibson, N., Spolander, G., & Yuill, C. (Eds.). (2023). *Social work: An introduction* (3rd edn). SAGE.

Maclean, S., Finch, J., & Tedam, P. (2018). *SHARE – A new model for social work.* Kirwin Maclean Associates Ltd.

Tedam, P. (2024). *Anti-oppressive social work practice* (2nd edn). Learning Matters.

Reference list

Bates, P., & Silberman, W. (2007). *Modelling risk management in inclusive settings.* National Development Team.

Bernard, C. (2022). *Intersectionality for social workers : A practical introduction to theory and practice.* Routledge.

Braye, S., & Preston-Shoot, M. (2016). *Practising social work law* (4th edn). Palgrave.

Braye, S., & Preston-Shoot, M. (2021). *Managing and supervising legal literacy in adult social work.* Research in Practice. ll-evidence-scope_final.pdf.

British Association of Social Workers (BASW). (2018). *Professional capabilities framework.* About the Professional Capabilities Framework (PCF) | BASW.

British Association of Social Workers (BASW). (2021). *Code of ethics.* BASW Code of Ethics for Social Work | BASW.

Brookfield, S. (2009). The concept of critical reflection: Promises and contradictions. *European Journal of Social Work, 12*(3), 293–304.

Brown, L., Moore, S., & Turney, D. (2014). *Analysis and critical thinking in assessment* (2nd edn). Research in Practice. Analysis and critical thinking in assessment: Resource Pack (2014) | Research in Practice.

Burnham, J. (2012). Developments in social GRRRAAACCEEESSS: Visible-invisible and voiced-unvoiced. In I. Knause (Ed.), *Culture and reflexivity in systemic psychotherapy: Mutual perspectives* (pp. 139–97). Karnac.

Burns, L., & Dallos, R. (2023). *Systemic practice (practice guidance).* CommunityCare InformChildren. Guide to applying systemic practice in social work.

Burton, V., & Revell, L. (2018). Professional curiosity in child protection: Thinking the unthinkable in a neo-liberal world. *The British Journal of Social Work, 48*(6), 1508–23.

Collingwood, P., Emond, R., & Woodward, R. (2008). The theory circle: A tool for learning and for practice. *Social Work Education, 27*(1), 70–83.

Davis, A., & Cree, V. E. (2006). *Social work : Voices from the inside.* Routledge.

Department for Education. (2023). *Working together to safeguard children 2023: A guide to multi-agency working to help, protect and promote the welfare of children.* Working together to safeguard children - GOV.UK.

Department of Health & Social Care. (2024). *Care and support statutory guidance.* Care and support statutory guidance - GOV.UK.

Domakin, A. (2022). *Defensible decision-making in children's social care: Resource Pack.* Research in Practice / Practice Supervisors Development Project (PSDP). ddm_resource-pack_web.pdf.

Earle, F., Fox, J., Webb, C., & Bowyer, S. (2017). *Reflective supervision: Resource pack.* Research in Practice. reflective_supervision_resource_pack_2017.pdf.

Fook, J., & Askeland, G. A. (2006). The "critical" in critical reflection. In S. White, J. Fook, & F. Gardner (Eds.), *Critical reflection in health and social care*(pp. 40–53) . Open University

Fook, J., & Askeland, G. A. (2007). Challenges of critical reflection: "Nothing ventured, nothing gained." *Social Work Education, 26*(5), 520–33.

Fook, J., & Gardner, F. (2007). *Practising critical reflection: A resource handbook.* Open University Press.

Glaister, A. (2008). Introducing critical practice. In S. Fraser & S. Matthews (Eds.), *The critical practitioner in social work and health care.* SAGE Publications.

IfATE (2023). *Social Worker.* Integrated Degree. Accessible here: https://www .instituteforapprenticeships.org/apprenticeship-standards/social-worker -integrated-degree-v1-1.

Institute for Apprenticeships and Technical Education (IfATE). (2018). *Social worker (integrated degree) - KSBs.* Social worker (integrated degree) / Institute for Apprenticeships and Technical Education.

Killick, C., & Taylor, B. (2024). *Assessment, risk & decision making in social work – An introduction* (2nd edn). Learning Matters.

Killion, J. P., & Todnem, G. R. (1991). A process for personal theory building. *Educational Leadership, 48*(6), 14–16.

Lewis, B., Pipe, C., & Bostock, L. (2022). *Systemic social work and contextual safeguarding – key messages for practice.* Contextual Safeguarding Programme at University of Durham. Systemic Social Work and Contextual Safeguarding | Contextual Safeguarding.

Luft, J., & Ingham, H. (1955). *The Johari window, a graphic model of interpersonal awareness.* Western Training Laboratory in Group Development at University of California.

Maclean, S., Finch, J., & Tedam, P. (2018). *SHARE – a new model for social work.* Kirwin Maclean Associates Ltd.

Maclean, S., & Harrison, R. (2015) *Theory and practice: a straightforward guide for social work students.* (3rd edn). Kirwin Maclean Associates Ltd.

Munro E. (2011). *The Munro review of child protection: Final report: A child-centred system.* The Stationery Office. Munro-Review.pdf.

Munro, E. (2020). *Effective child protection* (3rd edn). SAGE.

Parker, J. (2025). *Social work practice : Assessment, planning, intervention & review* (7th edn). Learning Matters.

Parkes, K. (2023). Risk assessment. In J. Lishman, J., Bolger, N. Gibson, G. Spolander, & C. Yuill (Eds.), *Social work : An introduction* (3rd edn). SAGE.

Preston-Shoot, M. (2019). *Making good decisions: Law for social work practice* (2nd edn). Macmillan International Higher Education.

Ruch, G. (2018). Theoretical frameworks informing relationship-based practice. In G. Ruch, D. Turney, & A. Ward (Eds.), *Relationship-based social work: Getting to the heart of practice* (2nd edn, pp. 37–54) . Jessica Kingsley Publishers.

Rutter, L., & Brown, K. (2020). *Critical thinking & professional judgement for social work* (5th edn). Learning Matters.

Sanderson, H., & Lewis, J. (2012). *A practical guide to delivering personalisation: Person-centred practice in health and social care.* Jessica Kingsley.

Schön, D. A. (1983/2016). *The reflective practitioner: How professionals think in action.* Routledge.

Shepherd, E. (2022). *Good practice in recording and access to records: Strategic briefing.* Research in Practice. Good practice in recording and access to records: Strategic Briefing (2022) | Research in Practice.

Social Work England (SWE). (2019). *Professional standards.* Professional standards - Social Work England.

Tedam, P. (2024). *Anti-oppressive social work practice* (2nd edn). Learning Matters.

Thacker, H., Anka, A., & Penhale, B. (2019). Could curiosity save lives? An exploration into the value of employing professional curiosity and partnership work in safeguarding adults under the Care Act 2014. *The Journal of Adult Protection, 21*(5), 252–67.

Thompson, S., & Thompson, N. (2023). *The critically reflective practitioner* (3rd edn). Bloomsbury Academic.

Turney, D. (2014). *Analysis and critical thinking in assessment (2nd edition): A literature review*. Research in Practice. Analysis and critical thinking in assessment: Literature review (2014) | Research in Practice.

Ward, A. (2018). The use of self in relationship-based practice. In G. Ruch, D. Turney, & A. Ward (Eds.), *Relationship-based social work: Getting to the heart of practice* (2nd edn, pp. 46–65) . Jessica Kingsley Publishers.

Wonnacott, J. (2014). *Developing and supporting effective staff supervision: A reader to support the delivery of staff supervision training for those working with vulnerable children, adults and their families*. Pavilion Publishing and Media Ltd.

9

Managing your well-being as a social work apprentice

Laura James

Chapter Outline

Your well-being as a priority   184
Stress   187
Emotional intelligence   188
Self-awareness   189
Vicarious trauma   190
Imposter syndrome   191
Time management and organizational skills   192
The support available to you   193
Engaging in supervision   194
Mindfulness   196
Chapter summary   199

This chapter will focus on the management of your well-being as a social work apprentice learner. Being a social work apprentice learner can be very challenging, and trying to find the right balance between work, study and personal life can be difficult, especially at the start of your apprenticeship journey . . . and during your whole social work journey too. This chapter will explore the notions of both self-awareness and emotional intelligence and will explore the importance of engaging in supervision and how to get the most out of supervision. This chapter will explore the support available to you from both training providers and organizations and will offer signposting to other useful services and tools. It is important to acknowledge, as noted in other chapters, that the support may differ between training providers and organizations across the country; however, the nature of the support will largely be very similar, and so whilst specific services will not be referenced, the types of different support you should be able to access will be examined.

Moreover, this chapter will support you to consider how you can seek support and manage competing priorities that arise during your apprenticeship. This chapter will consider the links between positive well-being and practice and will explore the idea of imposter syndrome. This chapter will share a range of supportive tools that can help with effective time management, and there will be a number of activities that you can undertake to increase your self-awareness and further develop your resilience. Finally, this chapter will include some case studies from real life apprentice learners, who will provide you with some top tips and also give you a true perspective of the reality of studying a social work apprenticeship.

Your well-being as a priority

Becoming an apprentice can be a daunting experience. Whether you have been employed in a different role within the same organization or whether you are new to the organization, you have become an apprentice in the journey that, as highlighted in the introductory paragraph, can be a challenging one. As an apprentice studying a towards a professional qualification at degree level, the expectations are high, and getting the balance right between studying, working full time and managing your home and personal life can often feel like a huge struggle. The good news is that a significant number of social work apprentices have been on this journey before you, and they have proved that the journey is possible.

During the pre-application stage, you may have talked to other apprentices and sought advice from your employer and training provider about how to manage all of what is expected, and you may even have felt that because of your organizational and time management skills, and the support you already have around you, that you are ready and able to brace the storm of the apprenticeship, so to speak. Regardless of this, there are often pinch points, usually at the beginning, halfway through and towards the end, whereby you may feel that things are tough and overwhelming, and you may even be considering whether the journey as an apprentice is in fact worth it. You may experience stress and feel that your well-being is not being prioritized because of all of the competing demands you are juggling. All of the feelings are totally normal and, I assure you, have been shared by so many former apprentices. Whilst these feelings are normal, ensuring you prioritize your well-being is crucial.

From the very beginning of the apprenticeship journey, it is important to be clear about your boundaries when it comes to your own well-being, as maintaining resilience will prevent you from faltering. Later on in this chapter, you will be introduced to different topics, approaches and exercises that will support you to think about how you can manage your well-being. The two case studies will provide you with real life perspectives from final-year social work apprentices who have shared the lessons they learned about managing their own well-being; you might wish to adopt some of the strategies they have shared.

Before the chapter examines the concepts detailed above, let's start with one of our apprentice case studies.

Social work apprentice case study written by Richard Flather (written at the time of being a final-year social work apprentice)

Studying on an apprenticeship has many pressures and stresses, including meeting the expectations of the job, course deadlines, studying and going on placement. I have found, at times, that these have been prioritized above my own well-being. I have missed social outings and changed holiday plans to fit around the apprenticeship; at times, when I have gone on holiday, there has been a sense of guilt that there is an essay due, or I have found my mind being occupied by cases. All too often, I have been on holiday sat in the hotel room or caravan at 5.00 am with a mountain of books or had the laptop open typing away before anyone was awake.

In the long run, this method of working is unsustainable, and you will find yourself reaching burnout far quicker and before you have started your social work post. Indeed, in the second year of my apprenticeship, there was a point when it started to overwhelm me, and my well-being was at an all-time low; thankfully, I was able to make it to the summer holidays where I could recover. In the third year of my apprenticeship, I decided that a different approach was needed if I was to maintain a good level of well-being and ultimately progress to social work.

As an apprentice, there is a sense that you want to do well and project an image that you can manage; however, this should not come at a cost of well-being. It is important to remember that you will not be able to perform as an apprentice if your well-being is compromised. For me, I found that supervision was vital to my well-being and to overcoming the fear of being open and honest about how I was coping. It is easy to think that if you admit you are not coping, it is a sign of weakness, but it is the opposite and a sign strength that you are asking for support and know your limitations. Adopting this attitude, I found myself requesting supervision to discuss my well-being, and in one instance, this resulted in an increase in my protected time during my work-based learning time to complete an essay.

Using support throughout the degree apprenticeship is essential to maintain well-being and a balance between academic, professional and personal commitments. At the university I am an apprentice at, there are a number of support groups, including academic skills support that can give support and advice on study skills. In addition, tutorial support is available, all of which can be used to manage the academic side of the apprenticeship, relieving some of the stressors of studying at this level. In the case of my cohort, a social media group was created for apprentices to discuss the course and offer advice and support, although it is helpful to remember that this can be harmful and must be managed. It is easy to start comparing yourself to others, and it must be remembered that it is your journey and that each journey is individual. Likewise, do not be disheartened if your grades or outcomes are not what you expect; use this as an opportunity to grow, learn and improve; no one is perfect.

For me, the biggest aspect of managing my own well-being was being organized; don't leave coursework or asking for support to the last possible chance. I found being organized allowed me to assign time to myself that was protected, and this enabled me to look after my own well-being. I set aside time each week to go the gym and an afternoon in the weekend to look after my well-being, meet friends and spend time with family without the guilt of closing the laptop, not thinking about cases or the course. This is not easy and is a skill that develops over time, but it enabled me to be more energized and motivated when retuning to the demands of the apprenticeship.

Stress

It is no secret that social work can be an incredibly stressful occupation, and it could be said that the stress associated with social work is one of the reasons why there continues to be a shortage of social workers nationally. Many surveys undertaken over the years suggest that whilst many social workers truly value their role, enjoy the positive impact they can have and are incredibly passionate about making a difference to people's lives, the role in itself can be very stressful. Social work is both a very demanding role yet is also a very rewarding one, and this is conveyed by social workers nationally. The rewarding aspect of the role is certainly what draws people to the profession.

Growing managerial requirements, along with the 'dichotomy of demand between value-based relational social work and evidence-based performance can bring about a lot of internal and external conflict to the practitioner who needs to reconcile both to daily working life' (Starns, 2022: 31). Logan (2014, cited in Starns, 2022) advocates that the experience of a social worker is one of strong emotional intensity that tests physical and psychological well-being to the full extent of personal limits. This advocation may indeed be a true reflection, and if you are working in a setting alongside social workers, you may very well have heard similar notions from them about the challenges and complexities of the role, and you may have observed directly how the role can cause stress to those undertaking it.

Whilst this may sound a little negative in one respect, as an apprentice, you have the opportunity to learn from those you work with and to reflect upon the impact of your role as an apprentice on your own stress levels. Often, stress is seen as a very negative thing; however, stress is a very normal part of life. Knowing what causes you to feel stressed and knowing how to manage your own stress (which will be very different to others) is the key to responding to it and to minimising the impact it has on your well-being. Whilst your role may differ significantly to that of your social work colleagues, it is fully acknowledged that the role of social work apprentices comes with its own stressors, and due to the challenge of juggling a full-time job, full-time study and a personal life, stress can become a familiar experience.

Reflective activity 9.1

Think about where you are in your apprenticeship journey. What stressors do you currently have that do or could impact your well-being? Can you identify three?

In the coming weeks, take time to observe a social worker colleague; what do you envisage their triggers for stress are? Can you identify three?

What strategies could you adopt to mitigate the impact on your well-being?

Emotional intelligence

The notion of emotional intelligence was considered in 1920 by Thorndike, who suggested that humans possessed a number of different intelligences; he referred to the skills of understanding and managing other people and acting wisely in human relations as a social intelligence (Thorndike, 1920). Others around the same time sought to advocate for a social intelligence but were, however, overlooked until the work of Gardner (1983) was brought into prominence. Gardner (1983) spent most of his career researching cognitive development and concluded that the established view of traditional intelligence was, in most parts, unjustifiable. Consequently, he advocated that were a number of unique intelligences which he described as a collection of discrete cognitive competencies. Gardner (1983) argued that only certain areas of a person's intelligence were challenged and tested through the use of psychometric testing, and intelligences, such as those now known as emotional intelligence, were disregarded until later in life, when they may have been required for certain employments, for example, in social work.

Goleman (2006) strongly agrees that emotional intelligence is the biggest indicator of human success and has been a more recent pioneer in the field. Goleman (2011) in his advocation also emphasizes the importance of social intelligence competencies, those being social awareness, empathy and social skills; he asserted that both emotional and social intelligences could be improved through repetition and education and, thus, could be taught. Years later on from these proposals, emotional intelligence, which is said to be the ability to understand oneself in order to understand others, is viewed to be a required intelligence within social work, and it is clear to see why, given the relational focus within social work.

As an apprentice, it is important to reflect upon your own emotional intelligence and to think about how you could enhance it further. The more you understand yourself, the easier it will be to understand others. Being emotionally intelligent can significantly improve your well-being, as being more self-aware allows you to develop strategies that will support you to manage your well-being. In turn, your practice will be more manageable, and the challenges you experience may become less stressful.

Self-awareness

It became apparent in the previous section that in order to be emotionally intelligent, you must be self-aware. The use of self is a key aspect of relationship-based practice (Howe, 2008). In order to be able to develop effective relationships with others and begin to understand their experiences, it is imperative that you know yourself first. Being aware of your own emotional state is essential if you are trying to relate to those in need. Howe (2008: 185) argues that 'the more emotionally aware the social worker is, the more connected they will be to those who use their services and the more open and accurate their responses and communications will be'.

Self-awareness is something that often needs developing and does involve a lot of self-reflection. It is easy to think that you know yourself well, but then you may often wonder why you might struggle to relate to others, or you might find yourself questioning the emotions of others; this is because, on the surface, we do often think we know ourselves well . . . why wouldn't we? The truth is, though, that it often takes deep reflection to truly understand ourselves. Once we know ourselves, it becomes much easier to understand our own triggers for stress and our barriers, and we become more emotionally intelligent.

The concept of self-awareness was explored in more detail in Chapter 7, and so it may be worth going back to Chapter 7 to think about how you can further develop your self-awareness through reflection.

Reflective activity 9.2

In order to enhance your emotional intelligence and develop your self-awareness further, here are some exercises you could try:

1. Write down three strengths you feel you have and three areas for development you feel you could work on.
2. Ask others (colleagues, friends, family) what they think about you: what do they think your strengths are; what do they think you could improve on? This will give you insight into how others (including those with lived experience) see you. If there were some surprises, how self-aware are you?
3. Write an action plan, considering the differences between how you view yourself and how others view you.

Vicarious trauma

It is becoming particularly prevalent that social workers can experience what is known as vicarious trauma; this is a secondary type of trauma derived from regular exposure to the trauma of others. Any type of trauma can impact a person's well-being, and as a social work apprentice, you will likely be containing the trauma experiences of those you are working with; all containers have their limits. This type of trauma can and is being experienced by social workers across the country; it is positive, though, that this type of trauma is more widely recognized now in social work, and organizations are thinking more about what this looks like, the impact of it and the support needed for social workers and other practitioners who are experiencing it.

I mention this here at this point in this chapter because I feel that being self-aware will support you to be able to identify this type of trauma and, thus, be able to seek the right support in response; this, in turn, will support you to manage your well-being. I think it is also pertinent to highlight here that your organization has a role to play in supporting you to manage this type of trauma, and through support mechanisms such as supervision, peer support and training, it would be useful for you think about the impact of vicarious trauma for you as a social work apprentice and future social worker and to work with your line manager and workplace mentor to identify the support you need to manage it.

Imposter syndrome

Urwin (2017) suggests that imposter syndrome is when someone experiences unwarranted feelings of inadequacy in relation to their own abilities; this can often be linked to self-efficacy, and those who experience imposter syndrome often doubt their own knowledge, skills and levels of experience and instead can sometimes think that their successes and achievements are down to luck rather than their own abilities (Community Care, 2023). Former social work apprentices and, indeed, those qualified and practising as social workers can and do experience imposter syndrome, and it can result in feelings of anxiety and uncertainty. Some apprentices have reported that they feel lucky to have gained a place on the apprenticeship given the benefits it brings; however, the reality is that it is your prior experience, transferable knowledge, relatable skills and the potential you demonstrated in your interview that resulted in you gaining a place on the social work apprenticeship.

Whilst experiencing imposter syndrome can often feel like the feeling is here to stay, there are ways you can overcome it. Firstly, sharing how you feel can help. Sharing your feelings within supervision, with your manager and with your workplace mentor can help to digest the reality of your achievements and where you are on your journey. Reflecting upon your journey so far and celebrating your successes that led you to be where you are can also help. This, of course, can be much easier said than done, as one of the shared challenges we often face as human beings is being able to identify our strengths and celebrating them. Moreover, cultivating self-compassion through mindfulness techniques can support you to overcome imposter syndrome. There are lots of mindfulness activities that are accessible on the internet that could support you to do this, and further on in this chapter, mindfulness is explored in some more depth. Finally, whilst probably the most difficult, accepting the feeling will help, as the chances are that even if you implement the techniques explored, later on in your career, you may experience imposter syndrome again (Abramson, 2021).

Time management and organizational skills

Whilst on the surface the skills of managing your time and being organized may sound straightforward, they can often get lost in the juggle of managing all of those competing priorities that have been discussed previously. The challenge of managing time comes in many forms; some examples include assignment writing, planning and submissions; caseload deadlines; recording your off-the-job training; and the commute to your training provider. In addition to these apprenticeship-specific tasks, you will experience the natural pressures of your job role; you will be mindful of the time spent with family and friends, the jobs that need doing around the house, the bills that need to be paid and, of course, the time you need to take for yourself in order to recharge and engage in self-care. All of these things need to be factored into your time management plans. A strict approach from the onset can give you both structure and boundaries, both of which will be invaluable to you on your apprenticeship journey.

Everybody has different ways in which they manage and cope with the different aspects of life (you will see some good examples in both of the case studies); however, the two things that consistently come up, when exploring the skills needed to manage the apprenticeship and everything that happens alongside it, are time management and being well-organized. Given the emphasis of these two skills, let's think about the different ways in which you could look to develop these.

- Diary management: whether this is electronic or paper, some apprentices find it useful to plan ahead. Documenting deadlines, off-the-job training days, working days, personal appointments and time for self-care in advance where possible is something that can be helpful in supporting you to structure your time and plan ahead. By setting out hours / days for self-care each week, you are setting healthy boundaries that will ensure your busy week is well-balanced.
- Daily planning: for some, it is helpful to visualize what each day will look like. Whilst this is similar to the diary management above, this idea instead looks at the specific focus of each day and may include tasks relating to the apprenticeship study element and the workplace and personal tasks for yourself. An example could be that in one day,

you plan to spend seven hours at work, one hour studying and one hour going to the gym.

- Time boxing: this involves allocating specific amounts of times to certain tasks; for example, you could allocate four hours on a Saturday to work on an assignment (no more, no less). This allows you to structure your plan and maintain focus given every task is very time specific.

- Action planning: whilst this may sound like an obvious method to support effective time management, it is probably one of the most widely used methods. Writing down actions and having goals is a great thing to do, as not only does this method make it clear to you what needs to be achieved and by when, it enables focus and clarity on the task at hand. The added bonus to action planning is that when the action is complete and the goal has been achieved, naturally, this offers a boost and a sense of accomplishment and so improves well-being too.

The support available to you

In previous chapters, the roles of those involved in supporting you have been introduced, and the remit of their roles has been explored. In addition to being able to access support from those named individuals (your employer, your workplace mentor and your training provider), there are other support services available to you. It is important to note here that whilst the names of the services may differ between employers and training providers, the remit of the support offered will be largely similar.

Firstly, you will have access to study skills support; this may be in the form of digital tools and guides, workshops online or in person, one-on-one tutorials or bookable training sessions. Each training provider may resource their study skills support slightly differently; however, there is likely to be accessible support focusing on assignment writing, referencing and presentation skills, to name a few. If you feel accessing study skills support would alleviate any worries you have and give you confidence in your abilities, then ask your training provider what this support looks like and how you can access it.

Secondly, as both an employee of your organization and an apprentice at your training provider you will have access to well-being services. Again, the types of support available within these well-being services will differ; however, types of support may include counselling, signposting to other services, well-being workshops such as managing stress and techniques to reduce anxiety, mental health drop-ins and crisis support. If you have a disability, a health need or learning support needs, or you think you might have, you will be able to access support both in your workplace and through your training provider either to be supported on an assessment pathway or so that appropriate adaptations can be implemented to ensure your learning experience is a positive one.

Engaging in supervision

Supervision is a requirement in social work settings, and it is likely that supervision is usual practice in the organization you work in. Supervision is fundamental to your journey as an apprentice and can be invaluable to your learning, development and your well-being. Supervision should be consistent, and you should be afforded the opportunity to receive supervision from someone whom with you can build a good working relationship, as this is also vital to the success of the supervisory relationship but also what is achieved from supervision itself.

Good quality supervision should be facilitated by those who have relevant experience and the necessary qualifications. Supervision is an essential tool that ensures accountably in decision-making as well as ethical practice (IFSW, 2012). Additionally, good supervision should support you to enhance your reflective and critical thinking skills (Carpenter et al., 2012). The frequency, structure and focus of supervision may differ across organizations and across the teams within your organization; however, as an apprentice, it is important that you are provided with regular and purposeful supervision during your apprenticeship. In your current role, you may have supervision whereby the main function is that of case management; it is crucial that your supervision as an apprentice includes time to focus on your learning, development and well-being too.

By having the protected time within supervision to talk about how you are managing, you are able to reflect in a safe space on your journey. Your manager or workplace mentor (or possibly both if you have supervision with both) will be able to support you within this space to think about how you can improve your well-being as a result of the reflections shared. Transparency is key, and so the more open you are about any challenges that are impacting your well-being, the more your manager or workplace mentor can do to support you. Actions that may arise from such discussions may include a reduction or a review of your caseload, more emphasis given on new learning, more focused time to engage in off-the-job training activities and / or having protected time for reflection.

In order to get the most out of supervision, having a supervision agreement or contract is very much encouraged. The agreement sets out the standing items that should form part of your supervision, and assessment and discussion of your well-being should always be a focus, especially given the emotionally fuelling role being undertaken by you as a social work apprentice. It is worth being mindful about the fact that, sometimes, agenda items can change to reflect your needs at the time of supervision; however, there should also be some core standing items so that the focus doesn't shift to become only one thing, for example, case management.

Top tip

- Ensure you have a supervision agreement or supervision contract. If you haven't got one, ask your workplace mentor for one.

Consideration of power is also important; it can often be felt by apprentices that there is a power imbalance in the relationship between you as the apprentice and the person facilitating supervision. If you feel this to be the case, it is important that you have the courage to raise this, as your supervision should be about you and your practice. One way to mitigate this is to jointly set out the supervision agenda and to work together to develop your supervision agreement. One other way in which you get the most out of your supervision is to prepare for it beforehand; think in advance about what you wish to explore, and this will support the structuring of discussions and will support you to feel more empowered.

Reflective thought

In order to feel more prepared for supervision, consider the main functions of your supervision and write down your thoughts ahead of your supervision session. In order to ensure your well-being takes precedence, it is a good idea to have your well-being at the very top of your supervision agenda, as this can influence discussions further on in the session.

Mindfulness

Mindfulness as a tool to support well-being has been growing in popularity over the last decade. Starns (2022) insinuates that whatever version of mindfulness is adopted, the practice of mindfulness is gaining traction in social work. Starns (2022: 1) suggests that because social work as a profession advocates for values of compassion, respect and kindness, mindfulness as a tool can be a natural ally of caring professions such as social work. It is acknowledged that, currently, research that seeks to explore the relationship between mindfulness and social work is in an embryonic stage; however, there are studies that do demonstrate the value of mindfulness in areas like social work (Starns, 2022).

Practising mindfulness can have many benefits to you as a busy social work apprentice; for example, it can support you to have a clearer mind and enable you to be calm, it can enhance your self-awareness, it can enhance your thinking, which can support effective decision-making, and it can support you to better understand and manage your emotions, which can have a positive impact on your responses in practice. Furthermore, practicing mindfulness can significantly improve the relationships formed with colleagues, other professionals and those with lived experience and, thus, can reduce any biases in your thinking (McGarrigle & Walsh, 2011).

Starns (2022) talks at length about the relationship between mindfulness and social work and explores the relationship between the Social Work England professional standards, the value base of social workers and the impact of mindfulness on achieving the professional standards and practising in an ethical value-based way. An example referred to is the professional standard statement of: valuing each person as an individual, recognizing their strengths and abilities. When considering the value of mindfulness, it could be said that this element of the professional standards can be achieved through being present in the moment, accepting and non-judgemental – all of which can be achieved through mindfulness.

Reflective activity 9.3

Read Chapter 1 of Starns (2022) and think about how mindfulness could benefit you as an apprentice. Think about the apprenticeship standard and the impact practising mindfulness could have on achieving each area of the knowledge, skills and behaviours statements.

Having thought about the benefits of mindfulness, are there elements you could adopt in your life to support you to manage your well-being? Could the benefits lead to a positive impact on your working, studying and personal life?

As the chapter is coming to an end, the following case study has been shared by another final-year social work apprentice. This apprentice talks about how her well-being has been managed during her apprenticeship journey and offers you some personal tips based on her experience.

Social work apprentice case study written by Katie Godwin (written at the time of being a final-year social work apprentice)

An apprenticeship, a degree, working full-time managing every day life . . . when you think of it that way, it sounds daunting, especially if you are like me and have never experienced university before; but what an opportunity. Three years of studying alongside everything else you already do; I'm sure many would think to themselves, 'How is that possible?' But believe me, it is, and you won't regret a second of it.

A good starting point is to think back to what you were doing three years ago (or at the point of starting your apprenticeship); it doesn't actually feel that long ago and doing the apprenticeship has made me realize time really does fly. Although there is pressure to meet deadlines and continue managing your normal working role, these are achievable and made so much easier by having a supportive employer who understands the apprenticeship scheme, allows for the required 'off-the-job' work and shows a real interest in your own progression.

I was lucky enough to complete my apprenticeship whilst working for a local authority who has supported a number of apprentices throughout their journey and provided plenty of opportunity to develop the knowledge, skills and behaviours required to complete the social work apprenticeship. The ups (and the downs, if there were any) could be discussed openly due to the positive relationships between apprentices, university and employers. I also think it is true to say that you make friends for life during your university years – the others completing the course who all have the same goal as you and the university staff who clearly want the best for you.

However, it is important to maintain your own well-being and recognize ways you can manage this throughout the duration of the programme, although these are likely to vary from person to person.

I thought I would share five of my top tips that I set in place from the start and continued throughout the three years of my apprenticeship:

1. Understand the deadlines, what is required and plan how this will be managed with other commitments you have.
2. Have time for yourself, don't give up what you enjoy, don't miss out on your favourite place, complete your favourite activity and plan and make it work. I set myself a rule, that I would not complete my work on a Sunday; that had always remained my family time, and three years later, that still remains the same.
3. Don't be hard on yourself; be kind and remember all the best made plans can go wrong, but by planning your time well, you can make adjustments as needed.
4. Don't put additional pressure on yourself. Throughout the apprenticeship, you will learn that you are better at some things than others; this also includes different models / assignment styles (whether it be an interview style or a critical reflection written piece); you will find your strengths and weaknesses.
5. Talk to others and use the services available at the university, such as apprentice support, librarians and academic skills support. They are there to help and offer great services. Also, remember your peers are having a similar experience; it's okay to ask for help.

I always found it was important to recognize the opportunity I was given whilst completing the apprenticeship, to gain the qualification to allow me to become a social worker whilst gaining vital experi-ence in the workplace but also having the opportunity and support to complete two placements in settings which I otherwise would not have had the opportunity to explore. We may all think we know which area of social work we want to work in, but having the opportunity to spend time in other areas may open your eyes to more options, even those we would not have previously considered.

If anyone asked me whether I would recommend the apprentice-ship, I could only say yes. To gain a qualification whilst having the work experience is brilliant; to build relationships with your employer who supports you and build relationships with the university makes the whole journey very enjoyable.

Chapter summary

This chapter has sought to explore the concept of well-being and has considered different ways in which your well-being can be managed as a social work apprentice. The concepts of stress and imposter syndrome have been examined, as both of these will likely be experienced in your journey as a social work apprentice and possibly beyond qualification too. The range of very different feelings you will feel on your journey are totally normal, and it is again normal to feel overwhelmed and deflated, particularly at certain points within your journey. What is hopefully reassuring to you is that there is a lot of support available to you both within your organization and through your training provider.

Your employer has invested in you to become an apprentice, and the team around you wants you to succeed. In addition to the support detailed, there are other supportive tools and activities which are easily accessible digitally; for example, there are questionnaires on emotional intelligence and action plans to complement your work, and there are also lots of fun and creative exercises that you can do to learn more about yourself in order to develop your self-awareness. The case studies included in this chapter have hopefully given you some real life insight into the experiences of apprentices, and the lessons learned and strategies shared should guide you in your own journey. Your well-being needs to be at the forefront of all you do, as it will be your resilience, dedication and motivation that see you through the journey ahead, and each of these traits requires your well-being to be intact.

Recommended reading

Howe, D. (2008). *The emotionally intelligent social worker.* Palgrave Macmillan.
Starns, B. (2022). *The mindful social worker: Living your best social work life.*
Critical Publishing.

References

Abramson, A. (2021). *How to overcome imposter phenomenon.* https://www.apa
.org/monitor/2021/06/cover-impostor-phenomenon.

Carpenter, J., Webb, C., Bostock, L., & Coomber, C. (2012). *Effective
supervision in social work and social care: SCIE research briefing no. 43.*
Social Care Institute for Excellence. www.scie.org.uk/publications/briefings
/briefing43.

Community Care. (2023). *How I overcame imposter syndrome as a social
worker and manager.* https://www.communitycare.co.uk/2023/06/20/how-i
-overcame-imposter-syndrome-as-a-social-worker-and-manager/.

Gardner, H. (1983). *Frames of mind: The theory of multiple intelligences.* Basic
Books.

Goleman, D. (2006). *Working with emotional intelligence.* Bantam Books.

Goleman, D. (2011). *The brain and emotional intelligence: New insights.*
Northampton. More than Sound LLC.

Howe, D. (2008). *The emotionally intelligent social worker.* Palgrave Macmillan.

IFSW. (2012). *Effective and ethical working environment for social work: The
responsibilities of employers of social workers.* International Federation of
Social Workers.

Logan, S. L. (2014). Meditation, mindfulness and social work. *Social Work
Journal for Women.* DOI: https://doi.org/10.1093/acrefore/9780199975839
.013.981.

McGarringle, T., & Walsh, C. A. (2011). Mindfulness, self-care and wellness
in social work: Effects of contemplative training. *Journal or Religion and
Spirituality in Social Work: Social Thought, 30*(3), 212–33.

Starns, B. (2022). *The mindful social worker: Living your best social work life.*
Critical Publishing.

Thorndike, R. K. (1920). Intelligence and its uses. *Harpers Magazine, 140,*
227–335.

Urwin, J. (2017). Imposter phenomena and experience levels in social work:
An initial investigation. *British Journal of Social Work, 48*(5), 1432–46.

10

Conclusion

Laura James

Chapter Outline

Some final top tips	204
Thank you and good luck	208

This book has sought to introduce some key concepts to you that we hope you will find helpful on your social work apprenticeship journey. Whilst there are certainly lots of valuable resources out there that seek to promote knowledge in the areas explored in this book, we hope that this book has been helpful in supporting you to frame the topics within a social work apprenticeship context. The first three chapters sought to introduce you to the apprenticeship standard and the knowledge, skills and behaviours, and the concept of assessment was explored. These chapters considered the changes to the standard in recent years, and the End Point Assessment, which is a core part of all apprenticeships, was examined. Chapter 2 sought to support you to think about the very beginning of the apprenticeship; for example, expectations were explored, and you were invited to think about how you could prepare for applying for and starting the apprenticeship, what your support network may look like and what your prior knowledge and experience looked like, as this very much influences your learning journey. Chapter 3 examined the apprenticeship standard in depth and gave you lots of ideas on how the knowledge, skills and behaviours can be applied during your studies.

Chapter 4 explored the somewhat tricky concept of applying theory and knowledge to practice. Whether you are at the very beginning, halfway through or even approaching the end of your social work apprenticeship journey, it is okay to feel overwhelmed by all of the knowledge you are being presented with. Applying your new knowledge to your work-based practice can often feel like a challenge, and sometimes, you may ask yourself what it is you should even be applying; however, with a little time, patience, practice and indeed support from those invested in your learning journey, you will find that applying your new learning does become a little easier, and you will certainly surprise yourself with how much you have retained and how your confidence in practice has increased. Quite often, it is the case that you were doing something in a certain way or have identified a reason as to why someone may present in a certain way; however, until you started your social work training, you may not have necessarily thought there was a named theory to explain and frame your thinking.

Chapter 5 introduced you to safeguarding from two different perspectives. Safeguarding is the 'bread and butter' of the social work role, so to speak; however, as a social work apprentice and, indeed, as a future qualified social worker, it is incredibly important to think how you can safeguard yourself. Understanding your own warning signs and knowing where to seek support is crucial. Sometimes, you may feel unsafe in practice, and you may feel anxious about undertaking certain tasks; knowing your organizational policies, engaging in supervision and practising good self-care will be of great benefit to you. Chapter 6 explored work-based learning in detail. Work-based learning is a significant part of the social work apprenticeship, and it is important that you are afforded both off- and on-the-job opportunities in the workplace; having the space in the workplace to apply your new learning will enable you to make good and steady progress against the apprenticeship standard, leading to full competency at the point of qualification. Chapter 6 also examined different approaches to 'placement' – across the country, training providers and employers will work in slightly different ways, and understanding how your training provider and employer work will enhance your understanding of how the placement element of social work training programmes is fulfilled.

Chapter 7 introduced you to the concept of reflection. Reflection is not only a key aspect of social work training but very much encouraged in social work practice. Developing the skill of reflection will support you in analysing each experience you have; by being able to unpack a situation through reflection, you will be able to identify how you can improve or enhance your future interventions. The chapter shared a number of different tools that you could try out on your apprenticeship journey; you are likely to find one that really works for you, and you may even use different ones to support you when reflecting upon different aspects of your practice. Chapter 8 explored the notion of critical thinking; this is a key skill needed in degree level study. By being able to critically think about different theoretical perspectives and aspects of your practice, you will be able to develop a much deeper understanding of your own practice, and your knowledge base will evolve and have more meaning when being applied in the workplace. Finally, Chapter 9 looked at the very important task of managing your well-being as a social work apprentice. The concept of well-being has been referred to in a number of the chapters, and this is because it is so important to ensure that your well-being is at the forefront of all you do. By effectively managing your well-being, you will be better able to manage the demands of the apprenticeship and will succeed. This chapter included two case studies from apprentices who shared their views on how they managed their own well-being, and some really useful top tips were shared too.

Reflective activity 10.1

Thinking about the topics discussed in each chapter and the stage you are at in your social work apprenticeship journey, can you think of three actions that would enhance your apprenticeship experience further?

Maybe you wish to enhance your critical thinking skills further, learn more about applying theory to practice, develop your reflection skills further or prioritize your well-being a little more?

SMART action planning will enable you to think about specific actions that are achievable and time focused. It is important to know what will have changed as a result of the action you have set. By knowing what the desired outcome is, you will be able to better visualize your goal, and this will motivate you to work on the actions you have set.

You may wish to use a template like the one below, and it may be a good idea to share this in your next supervision with your workplace mentor.

What do I need to do / know more about?	How can I achieve this?	When do I need to achieve this by?	How will I know I have achieved it? What will have changed?

Some final top tips

Most chapters have shared top tips about different things relating to the topics discussed in those chapters. Whether you are just embarking upon your social work apprenticeship journey, are part-way through or even approaching the end of your apprenticeship, here are some final top tips that you may find helpful:

Accessing support

As a social work apprentice, you are in a unique position as there are a number of key individuals who are invested in your apprenticeship journey. Make sure you take up their support and ask them for help when you need it. Don't feel as though you need to wait until supervision with your workplace mentor or a progress review with your university tutor. Moreover, if you ever feel as though you need to access additional services through either your employer or your training provider. . . . Do access them! Whether you feel you may need additional support in relation to your academic writing or whether you feel you are struggling to manage your well-being, reach out to the services, as they are there to support you. If you have or feel that you have a learning support need or disability, share this and access the right support as soon as possible, as appropriate adaptations can be implemented in both your workplace and the classroom and you may also be able to access some really helpful software to support your learning.

Keeping up with the demands of additional apprenticeship tasks

You will have apprenticeship-specific tasks to complete alongside your academic module work. It is important that you keep on top of these tasks as they can soon build up. Apprenticeship progress is subject to regular compliance checks to ensure that training providers are adhering to the apprenticeship funding rules; therefore, it is much better to remain on track to avoid being reminded to catch up. Should there be a gap in your off-the-job training recording, a break in learning may be initiated; this can be avoided by keeping your recordings up to date and will ensure that the duration of your apprenticeship is not extended unnecessarily. You may find it useful to dedicate one evening a week where you can add the week's off-the-job training recording and complete any other tasks that are specific to your apprenticeship.

Managing your time

At the very beginning of your apprenticeship journey, you may find it a real challenge to get the balance of managing a full-time job, home life, caring responsibilities and degree level study right. Feeling this way at the beginning is totally normal. You were already busy prior to becoming a social work apprentice, and now you have taken on degree level study, which is demanding in itself. The reassuring thing is that it does get easier as the apprenticeship goes on, and you develop some kind of internal resilience as you pave your way through your apprenticeship studies. Managing your time is absolutely vital; planning out your time in advance is helpful as you can prepare yourself for the things that are due to occur, for example, assignment deadlines. You may find using a diary or time planner helpful, as this can visually support you to manage your time. It is important that you make time for yourself and your family and that you prioritize this time. Within Chapter 9, Katie Godwin, who wrote one of the case studies, talks about choosing a day each week to not do any apprenticeship work. Katie stuck to this throughout her apprenticeship, and this supported her to manage her time and her well-being too.

Don't compare yourself to others

This is easier said than done; however, it is important that you try not to compare yourself to others. You may find that you begin to compare your assignment grades and your apprenticeship progress with others in your cohort; this can really get you down if you feel like others are achieving and making progress and you are not. It is important to remember that everyone has a different starting point, and some have studied at degree level before. Everyone learns in slightly different ways, too, and so some people may do better in a written assignment compared to a presentation or work-based portfolio. The opportunities given within the workplace may also differ at different times, and so sometimes, you may make significant progress, and other times, your progress may be steady. So long as you are making progress against the apprenticeship standard at each progress review point, then believe you are where you need to be and making the progress you are supposed to be making. Please do also consider accessing academic skills support, coaching or additional support in the workplace if you do feel you need some additional support to help you make even more progress than you are currently are.

Applying theory to practice

Throughout this book in different ways, the concept of applying theoretical knowledge to your practice has been explored. There are undeniably so many theories that you will be introduced to throughout your apprenticeship journey, and it can feel overwhelming at times. Use the different models introduced in this book to begin to apply one theory at a time. During the protected study time you give yourself, try applying one theory at a time through critical reflection activities. Once you have understood that theory and have grasped how to apply it in practice, move on to practice applying the next one. Nobody expects you to be well versed in all thing's theory in your first year, and the truth is, you will still be very much learning in year three as you will continually be introduced to new theories. Remember . . . a theory is a means of explaining something, and for you, theories can help in supporting you to understand what is going on for the person with lived experience that you are supporting.

Reflect to learn

You are continually learning as an apprentice. Developing as a reflective practitioner will support your learning process and will allow you to learn more about yourself. Have a go at using some of the tools and models shared in Chapter 7 of this book and see what you can learn about yourself and your practice. By engaging in reflection, you can identify how you could do things differently; this often leads to improved practice and increased confidence too.

Applying the apprenticeship standard

The best way to learn about the standard and apply it is to start referring to it regularly. Each time you reflect upon something, think about which knowledge, skills and behaviours were relevant. As you prepare for each of your progress reviews, think clearly about which KSBs you have developed. If you do this regularly, by the time you reach your End Point Assessment period, you will be able to confidently articulate your competency against each area of the apprenticeship standard.

Enjoy the journey

This one is simple but may not be easy at times. The reality of studying the social work apprenticeship is that it really is hard work, stretching and challenging, but what we know from all of those who qualified before you is that it is very rewarding and humbling and a worthwhile journey that is often life-changing with respect to the increase in confidence and resilience that it gifts you. You will learn so much and so quickly, and you will form friendships that will last beyond your studies. You will share difficult times with your peers and find yourself questioning why you embarked upon this journey when you are working late at night on your assignments or struggling to comprehend what a certain piece of literature may say. All of this said, you will find so much joy in the many opportunities the apprenticeship will give you. Enjoy each single moment, as it truly does go by so quickly.

Reflective activity 10.2

What are your top three top tips from the book? Write them down so you remember what they are and so you can begin to implement them.

1.
2.
3.

Thank you and good luck

I wanted to conclude this chapter and this book by saying thank you.

Thank you for choosing this book and for taking the time to read the chapters within it. The authors selected for this book were selected because they have real life experience of the social work apprenticeship. Each of the authors has either taught, supported, or been a social work apprentice. Many have been involved in the delivery of social work apprenticeships from the apprenticeship's inception. I felt it was incredibly important for those writing the book to have had relevant experience of the social work apprenticeship as I feel the content, along with the top tips shared, are a genuine insight, and I hope this came across to you. I hope you found the plethora of reflective activities useful. These were designed to support you to think about each of the chapter topics in small chunks so that learning would become easier and so that different concepts were understandable and clear. I am very pleased to have included two case studies within Chapter 9 from real social work apprentices; both of these apprentices managed their journey well, and I would encourage you to think about how you could apply at least some of what they both shared.

Wherever you may be on your social work apprenticeship journey, I wish you the very best of luck. Remember, the journey will be a challenge, but success is absolutely possible, and you are more than capable of achieving. This journey will not only develop your confidence but will increase your personal and professional resilience too. Resilience is very much needed in social work, and the apprenticeship builds it in abundance.

Here's to you . . . Our social workers of the future.

Glossary

Apprentice This is a term used for those studying an apprenticeship.

Apprenticeship standard The national occupational standard for your apprenticeship that encompasses the knowledge, skills and behaviours you are required to meet in order to achieve your apprenticeship. All apprenticeships in England have an approved apprenticeship standard.

Employer This term is used to describe the organization at where an apprentice is employed. Throughout this book, reference is made to the employer and sometimes to the organization. They are used interchangeably.

IfATE The abbreviation for the Institute for Apprenticeships and Technical Education. Currently, this institute is involved in developing, reviewing and revising apprenticeship standards.

KSBs The abbreviation used for the knowledge, skills and behaviours (which form the apprenticeship standard)

Ofsted The Office for Standards in Education, Children's Services and Skills. Ofsted inspect providers who provide education and skills for learners of all ages. A key remit of inspection is apprenticeships.

Off-the-job training Refers to new learning and accounts for approximately 20 per cent of your training (a minimum of 6 hours recorded each week is required, in line with the apprenticeship funding rules).

On-the-job training Refers to training received from an employer in order for an apprentice to undertake the role they were employed to do.

Placement A focused period of time where those undertaking social work training undertake social work activities in order to develop competency against competency frameworks, such as the PCF and the apprenticeship standard.

Practice Educator Someone who formally assesses your practice during your time on placement. This is a different role to your workplace mentor.

PCF The abbreviation used for BASW's Professional Capabilities Framework. This framework is usually referred to during placement periods.

Social Work England Social Work England, sometimes abbreviated to SWE, is the regulator for social work in England.

Training provider The term is used by the Education, Skills and Funding Agency to define the organization providing the off-the-job training / academic qualification aspect of the apprenticeship. The training provider is usually a university and sometimes referred to as a higher education institution.

Those with lived experience This term used to describe those who have experience of using services / being in receipt of support. This book uses this term; however, other similar terms include 'experts by experience' and 'service users'. One particular model in Chapter 4 refers to the term 'service user', as this was part of the model name at the time of the model being introduced.

Workplace mentor The person in your organization who will support you during your apprenticeship, providing you with supervision, guidance and learning opportunities so that you make the required progress to achieve full competency of the apprenticeship standard. This person is usually a qualified and registered social worker.

Appendices

Appendix 1: The occupational duties of the social work apprenticeship standard and the knowledge, skills and behaviours.

Accessible here:

https://www.instituteforapprenticeships.org/apprenticeship-standards/st0510-v1-1

Occupation duties

Duty 1 Promote the rights, strengths and well-being of people, families and communities to ensure their voice and expertise is heard and acknowledged.

Duty 2 Be an accountable professional, acting in the best interests of people that use services by valuing each person as an individual and promoting their rights and by recognizing strengths and abilities.

Duty 3 Recognize differences across diverse communities and challenge the impact of disadvantage and discrimination on people and their families and communities.

Duty 4 Establish and maintain the trust and confidence of people so as to develop professional relationships that ensure they understand the role of a social worker in their lives.

Duty 5 Practise in ways that demonstrate empathy, authority and professional confidence and enable people to fully participate in discussions and decision-making.

Duty 6 Work directly with individuals and their families through the professional use of self, using interpersonal skills to develop relationships based on openness and transparency.

Duty 7 Actively listen to understand people, using a range of appropriate communication methods to build relationships.

Duty 8 Manage situations of potentially conflicting or competing values, and, with guidance, recognize, reflect on and work with integrity with ethical dilemmas.

Duty 9 Be accountable for quality practice and decisions made whilst working within legal and ethical frameworks, using professional authority and judgement appropriately and respectfully.

Duty 10 Select and use appropriate frameworks to assess, give meaning to, plan, implement and review effective interventions and evaluate the outcomes, in partnership with service users.

Duty 11 Apply knowledge and skills to address the social care needs of individuals and their families – commonly arising from physical and mental ill health, disability, substance misuse, abuse or neglect – to enhance quality of life and well-being.

Duty 12 Recognize the risk indicators of different forms of abuse and neglect and their impact on individuals, their families or their support networks and prioritize the protection of children and adults in vulnerable situations.

Duty 13 Work with relevant colleagues and agencies to support people experiencing difficult situations, to gather information and to make timely decisions when positive change is not evident.

Duty 14 Maintain accurate and timely records and reports in accordance with applicable legislation, protocols and guidelines to support professional judgement and organizational responsibilities.

Duty 15 Recognize professional limitations and how and when to seek advice from a range of sources, including named supervisors, senior social workers and other professionals. Make effective use of opportunities to discuss, reflect upon and test multiple hypotheses.

Duty 16 Maintain and record professional development and knowledge of social work practice. Use supervision and feedback to inform and critically reflect on practice and values, and the impact they have on practice.

Duty 17 Confidently fulfil statutory responsibilities, work within regulatory and organizational remit and contribute to its development.

Duty 18 Social workers must use technology, social media or other forms of electronic communication lawfully, ethically and in a way that does not bring the profession into disrepute and ensure their skills in this area are maintained and used to improve practice.

Duty 19 Act safely, respectfully and with professional integrity; promote ethical practice; and report concerns.

KSBs

Knowledge

K1: The importance of rights, responsibilities, freedom, authority and use of power.

K2: The importance of maintaining, and the limits of, confidentiality.

K3: That relationships with individuals and their carers should be based on respect, honesty and integrity.

K4: How to develop relationships appropriately.

K5: The impact of different cultures and communities and how this affects social work.

K6: Current legal and ethical frameworks.

K7: The concepts of participation, advocacy, co-production, involvement and empowerment.

K8: The contribution that peoples' own resources and strengths can bring to social work.

K9: The impact of different societies' views on human behaviour.

K10: The value of research and analysis, and be able to evaluate evidence to inform practice.

K11: That experiences and feelings affect behaviour in interactions.

K12: Social work theory, models and interventions; human growth and development across the lifespan; and the impact of key developmental stages and transitions.

K13: The impact of injustice, demography, social inequality, policies and other issues which affect the demand for social work services.

K14: How to update knowledge to ensure evidence-informed practice.

K15: The scope and limits of practice and when / how to seek advice from a range of sources.

K16: Models of supervision, critical reflection and self-reflection to enhance / change practice.

K17: Your employer's organizational context and systems and the impact on your practice.

K18: The concept of leadership and its application to practice.

K19: The requirements of the relevant professional body.

K20: Applicable safeguarding / health and safety legislation, policies and procedures.

K21: How to maintain your own personal safety and that of others in complex situations.

K22: Signs of harm, abuse and neglect and the importance of professional curiosity when these are observed and the appropriate risk assessment tools and processes to use.

K23: The role of the Social Worker and roles of others within safeguarding, appropriate to levels of skills and experience.

K24: The range of communication methods available to meet specific needs (both verbal and non-verbal).

K25: The importance of the impact of verbal and non-verbal communication.

K26: How communication skills affect the assessment of, and engagement with, individuals and their families / carers.

K27: The range of factors that affect effective communication, e.g. age, capacity, learning ability and physical ability.

K28: The full range of interpersonal skills required to work with other professionals and agencies.

K29: The different social and organizational contexts within which social work operates.

K30: The applicable legislation, policies and procedures,

K31: The principles of good recording and record keeping.

K32: The types, and benefits, of assistive technology.

K33: How to use relevant software applications.

K34: IT data sharing protocols.

K35: The potential misuses of technology, e.g. social media.

Skills

S1: Ensure professional ethical standards are developed, maintained and promoted.

S2: Take responsibility for your decisions and recommendations.

S3: Be aware of the impact of your own values on practice.

S4: Exercise authority as a Social Worker within the appropriate legal and ethical frameworks.

S5: Ensure the highest standard of person-centred approach so that people are treated with dignity and their rights, values and autonomy are respected.

S6: Practise in a non-discriminatory manner.

S7: Hear the views of people who use services, carers, their families and communities; recognize their expertise; and enable their views to have validity and influence.

S8: Promote the best interests of people who use services, carers, their families and communities.

S9: Work with people to enable them to make informed decisions and exercise their rights.

S10: Work to promote individual growth, development and independence.

S11: Undertake assessments of need and / or capacity.

S12: Initiate resolution of issues and use initiative.

S13: Gather, analyse, critically evaluate and use research information and knowledge in your practice to develop an understanding of the individual's situation.

S14: Make and receive referrals appropriately.

S15: Use social work methods, theories and models to enable individuals to identify actions to achieve change and improve life opportunities.

S16: Manage and weigh up competing / conflicting values or interests to make reasoned professional judgements.

S17: Work within scope of practice as an autonomous professional.

S18: Maintain high standards of personal and professional conduct.

S19: Manage the physical and emotional impact of your practice.

S20: Identify and apply strategies to build professional and emotional resilience.

S21: Use supervision to support and enhance the quality of your practice.

S22: Maintain your own health and well-being.

S23: Recognize the need to manage workloads and resources effectively.

S24: Keep your skills, knowledge and ongoing professional development up to date.

S25: Show an awareness of current and relevant legislation.

S26: Use a range of research methodologies to inform your practice.

S27: Work in partnership with others.

S28: Balance appropriate levels of autonomy within a complex system of accountability.

S29: Respond appropriately to unexpected situations; identify and challenge practices which present a risk to, or from, people you are working with, their carers or others in order to uphold professional requirements.

S30: Respond appropriately to signs of harm, abuse and neglect.

S31: Establish and maintain personal and professional boundaries.

S32: Follow health and safety policies and procedures.

S33: Communicate in English at the level required by Social Work England.

S34: Communicate your role and purpose sensitively and clearly, using appropriate language and methods.

S35: Communicate in a way which is engaging, respectful, motivating and effective, even when dealing with conflict or resistance to change.

S36: Exercise professional curiosity.

S37: Have difficult conversations with empathy.

S38: Demonstrate effective interpersonal skills.

S39: Engage with individuals and their families / carers and sustain effective relationships in order to effect change.

S40: Engage effectively in inter-professional and inter-agency working to achieve positive outcomes.

S41: Support networks, groups and communities to meet needs and outcomes.

S42: Maintain accurate and complete records in accordance with applicable legislation, protocols and guidelines.

S43: Prepare formal reports in line with legislation, policies and procedures.

S44: Critically reflect on / review practice and record the outcomes of reflection appropriately.

S45: Present reports in formal settings.

S46: Use technology to manage your work.

S47: Use technology to communicate appropriately.

S48: Maintain individuals' information security and protect data.

S49: Advise people on how to use assistive technology.

S50: Promote the use of technology to achieve better outcomes.

Behaviours

B1: Communicate openly, honestly and accurately. Listen to people and apply professional curiosity to evaluate and assess the information needed to provide quality advice, support or care.

B2: Treat people with compassion, dignity and respect and work together to empower positive change.

B3: Adapt your approach according to the situation and context.

B4: Commit to continuous learning within social work, with curiosity and critical reflection.

B5: Adhere to the Social Work England Standards of Conduct.

(IfATE, 2023)

Index

academic modules   4, 23, 24
academic qualification   22, 28
action planning   66, 193
affective forecasting   69
Ainsworth, Mary   60
Allain, L.   75
analytical assessment   173
anchoring effect   163
anti-oppressive practice   33, 134, 135,
    167, 178
apprentice learner   6, 17, 25, 28,
    39–41, 44, 52, 53, 55, 73, 104, 113,
    115–16, 183
apprenticeship   7, 8, 18, 38, 39, 42, 49,
    156, 169, 205; *see also* social work
    apprenticeship
  curriculum   4
  in England   3
  funding rules   50, 103, 205
  off-the-job training   8, 10, 11
  on-the-job training   8
  programme   3, 4, 10, 13, 21, 28, 104
  social workers   2, 3
  standard   4–7, 10, 56, 106, 144, 207
  stretch and challenge   52–4
  studies   18, 185, 192
artificial intelligence (AI)   88
Askeland, G. A.   133, 160
assessment   4, 22, 23, 25, 42, 53, 66, 90,
    105, 106, 173, 174
attachment theory   60, 61, 65, 66

bandwagon effect   163
Bassot, B.   75, 113
BASW   9, 26, 93, 114, 116, 117, 156,
    159, 164

Beddoe, L.   138
Bernard, C.   165
bias/biases   97, 129, 131, 149, 163, 171,
    178
Bowlby, J.   60, 65
Bratt, S.   132
Bretherton, I.   65
British values   16, 31–3
Brookfield, S.   162, 166
Brown, K.   155, 162, 163
Brown, L.   173
Burnham, J.   165
Burns, L.   160
Burton, V.   161

Care Act   46–8, 54, 158
Centrepoint   75
Child Protection Conference   108
Children Act 1989   54, 176
Clarke, N.   135
Coalition Government   32
Collingwood, P.   169
confirmation bias   163
continued professional development
    (CPD)   144
Cottrell, S.   135, 141
Cree, V. E.
    *Social Work: Voices from the
    Inside*   158
critical analysis   12, 154
critical incident analysis   142
critical reflection   131, 133, 139, 144,
    156, 162
  components   132
  SHARE model   157, 158, 166
  in social environment   159

critical thinking   12, 64, 131, 134, 154,
    178, 203
  analytical assessment   173
  anchoring effect   163
  assumptions   162
  bandwagon effect   163
  confirmation bias   163
  4D2P framework   167
  hindsight bias   163
  legal literacy   174
  power and privilege   167
  risk assessment (see risk assessment)
  in social work values   164–6
  systemic approach   160–2
  towards knowledge   170
culturagram   167

daily planning   192–3
Dallos, R.   160
Davies, K.   72
Davis, A.
  Social Work: Voices from the
    Inside   158
Davys, A.   138
decide   167
decision-making   11, 27, 96, 177
Department for Education   32
Dewey, J.   129, 133
diary management   192
discover   167
discrepancy matrix   172
discuss   167
disrupt   167
Douglas, V.   90
Driscoll, J.J.   145

Education and Training Standards   6, 8,
    20, 21, 33
Education Inspection Framework   32
Einstein   67
emotional intelligence   12, 135, 183,
    188–9, 199
empathic imagination   68

End Point Assessment (EPA)   4, 10, 17,
    24, 30, 34, 38, 39, 55, 207
England   2, 3, 6, 33
English skills   18
Enhanced Criminal Record
    Disclosure   19
ePortfolio   50, 52, 56
ethical awareness   93
ethical practice   11, 81
ethical tension   11, 27, 93, 95, 96, 98

Fahlberg, V.   65
feedback strategy   23, 105, 110–11, 140
Flather, Richard   9
Fook, J.   131, 133, 156, 159, 160, 162, 166
Ford, R.   132
formative assessments   23
4D2P framework   167
Fourie, J.   90
Freudenberger, H. J.   135
functional skills   10, 16–18

Gardner, H.   156, 159, 160, 162, 166,
    188
Gateway Review meeting   55
Glaister, A.   154
Godwin, Katie   9, 197, 206
Goleman, Daniel   135, 188
Grant, L.   135, 138
Gray, M.   72
group reflective sessions   140

Harrison, R.   160
Hennessey, R.   73
Hill, D.   63
hindsight bias   163
HM government   66
holy grail   176, 177
Howe, David   63, 189
human dignity   93

imposter syndrome   191, 199
information gathering   91

Ingham, H.   136
Institute for Apprenticeships
        and Technical Education
        (IfATE)   38–41
interdisciplinary working   109
intersectionality   165, 178

Johari window   136, 168
Jones, S.   132
Jung, C. G.   74

Killick, C.   164, 174
Killion, J.   130, 168
Kinman, G.   135, 138
knowledge, skills and behaviours
        (KSBs)   19, 28–30, 39–42, 44, 53,
        144, 156, 158, 164, 169, 207
    behaviour component   43
    knowledge component   43
    skills component   43
knowledge and skills statements
        (KSS)   6, 43, 116, 117
Knowles, M.   143

Laming, L.   133
learning from others   110
legal literacy   174
lens of intersectionality   165
level descriptors   115, 116
Lewis, B.   162
Lewis, J.   176
local authorities   17, 22, 158, 198
Logan, S. L.   187
Luft, J.   136

Maclean, Siobhan   62, 128–30, 143,
        146, 147, 155, 157, 158, 160, 166,
        169, 171, 178
Mantell, Andy   128, 135, 136, 140, 142
Mental Health Act   159
mentoring session   30, 122, 144, 168
Mezirow, J.   133
Miller, L. M.   73

mindfulness   191, 196–7
Munro, E.   163, 174–6

new learning   8, 21, 44, 46, 53, 107,
        141, 202
NHS   17, 22

observing   108, 109
off-the-job training   8, 10, 11, 24, 46,
        49–50, 52, 76, 103–4, 106, 107
    activities   50, 51
    record   51, 52
    rules   106
on-the-job training   8, 49, 103

Parker, J.   167, 168
placement   21, 47, 116, 202
    activities   121
    model   118–19, 124
    practice   104
    progress   120–1
    rotational placements   119–20
    shadowing placements   120
    virtual placements   120
practice educator   44, 53, 116, 121
professional boundaries   81, 84–8
professional capabilities framework
        (PCF)   9, 93, 114, 115, 117, 135,
        156
professional curiosity   43, 136–7, 161,
        178
professional identity   10, 25–6, 34, 104
professional judgement   94, 96–7, 173
progress reviews   18, 32, 44–6, 56, 107,
        111, 114, 139, 204
Protective Behaviours (PB)   82

Rankine, M.   139
reflection   11, 52, 127–9, 137, 138, 142,
        144, 202
    barriers to   142–3
    critical reflection (see critical
        reflection)

models of   130, 131, 145, 149
reflection for action   130
reflection in action   130
reflection on action   130–1
self-awareness   135–6
in social work practice   73
reflective framework   145–6
reflective log   52, 59, 140–1
reflective practice   128, 129
critical incident analysis   142
group reflective sessions   140
logs and journals   140–1
professional curiosity   136–7
reflective framework   145–6
reflective supervision   138
reflective tools   145–8
supervision session   138
use of self   73, 85, 168, 178, 189
weather model   147–8
reflective social workers   11, 128
reflective supervision   138, 161
reflective thinking   130
reflexive approach   168
reflexivity   168
Revell, L.   161
risk assessment
balancing benefits and harms   174–5
children and families   176
contextualizing behaviour   177
decision-making   177
informed risk taking   176
learning culture   177
person involvement   176
proportionality   176–7
tolerable risk   177
Rolfe, G.   68
Romeo, Lyn   161
rotational placements   119–20
Ruch, G.   160
Rutter, L.   142, 155, 162, 163

safeguarding   11, 81, 82, 89–90, 97, 98
Safeguarding Adult Reviews   161

safety   70, 82, 88
Sanderson, H.   176
Savage, Jordan   9
Schon, Donald   128, 130, 168
Scottish Social Services Council
    (SSSC)   87
Scragg, Terry   128, 135, 136, 140, 142
self-assessment   19, 28, 41, 42, 46, 47
self-awareness   12, 73, 105, 135–6, 156,
    183–4, 189, 199
self-care   136, 192
Serious Case Reviews   137, 161
shadowing   106, 108, 109
shadowing placement   120
SHARE model   157, 158, 166, 171, 178
Shaw, H.   110
Sheridan, M.   66
Sinek, Simon   146
skills days   119
Skills England   5
SMART action planning   143, 203
Smith., M.   110
social care worker   42, 54
Social Graces model   165, 167
social intelligence   188
social media   87–9
social work   2, 82, 96, 187
apprentice learners   59, 68
apprenticeship route   2
apprenticeship standard   4, 5, 7
curriculum   8
degree apprenticeship   8, 9
education   3
journey   86
learning   61, 65
practice   73, 93, 127–8, 155
practitioners   164, 171
programmes   6, 23, 28, 104
reflection   11
services   2
students   27, 44
theory   23, 91
values   11, 164, 166

social work apprenticeship   1, 8, 9, 85,
    87–90; *see also individual entries*
    academic modules   23
    academic qualification   22
    accessing support   204–5
    additional apprenticeship task   205
    application process   16–17, 19
    assessment   90
    British values   31–3
    case study   185–6, 197–9
    critical analysis   12
    critical thinking   12
    functional skills   16–18
    knowledge and skill statements   92
    new learning   21
    occupation duties   40
    professional identity   25–6
    professional judgement   96–7
    progress reviews   44–6
    risk management   91
    self-assessment skill   19
    vs. social work student   27–9
    theoretical knowledge to
       practice   206–7
    time management   205–6
    well-being management   12
    work-based learning   11
    workplace mentor   30
Social Work Degree Apprenticeship
    (SWDA)   1–3, 8, 9, 25, 31,
    37–40, 44, 46, 47, 51–3
Social Work England (SWE)   4, 6–9,
    18, 20, 25, 33, 40, 44, 52, 55, 84,
    110, 115, 119, 156, 158, 159, 196
    professional standard   114, 117
    Qualifying Education and Training
       standards   21
    reflection   144
    requirements for registration   21
    social work programmes   23
social worker apprenticeship
    standard   39, 55, 139, 144

social workers   26, 27, 54, 85, 88–90,
    93, 94, 96, 110, 123, 136, 143, 156,
    164, 191
    apprenticeship   2, 3, 93
    in England   2, 6
    reflective social worker   128
    use of self   73
Social Work: Voices from the Inside (Cree
    & Davis)   158
Socrates   154
Starns, B.   196, 197
Stone, C.   26, 123
Straussuer, Shulamith Lala
    Ashenberg   74
stress   185, 187, 189, 199
supervision   67, 137–9, 186, 194–5
    agreement   195
    group/peer supervision   131
    session   46, 122, 138, 168
SWOT analysis   113
systemic practice   160–2

Taylor, B.   164, 174
Tedam, P.   165, 167, 174
Thacker, H.   161
theory to practice   59, 61, 64, 75, 91,
    104, 169, 206–7
Thomas, G.   60
Thompson, N.   25, 26, 128, 129, 135,
    166, 170
Thompson, S.   128, 129, 166, 170
Thorndike   188
time boxing   193
time management   184, 192–3, 205–6
Todnem, G.   130, 168
Trailblazer Group   38–40, 43, 55
training providers   4, 5, 8, 17, 19–25,
    49, 106, 116, 121, 123, 184, 193,
    205

Urwin, J.   191
use of self   73, 85, 168, 178, 189

vicarious trauma   129, 190–1
virtual placements   120

weather model   147–8
well-being management   12, 136, 183,
        203
    action planning   193
    daily planning   192–3
    diary management   192
    emotional intelligence   183, 188–9
    imposter syndrome   191, 199
    mindfulness   196–7
    self-awareness   184, 189, 199
    stress   187, 199
    supervision   194–5
    support services   193–4
    time boxing   193
    transparency   195
    trauma experience   190–1
White, J.   160
WHY question   155
Williams, J.   131
Williams, S.   142
Wonnacott, J.   172
work-based learning   11, 102, 202
    activities   121
    continuous learning   106–7

feedback strategy   110–11
interdisciplinary working   109
knowledge and skills
        statements   116, 117
mentoring session   122
new learning   107
observing   108
off-the-job training   103–4
on-the-job training   103
opportunities   105, 112–13
placement model   118–19, 124
professional capabilities
        framework   114–17
progress on placement   120–1
reflect upon prior learning   113
rotational placements   119–20
rules, off-the-job training   106
shadowing   108
shadowing placements   120
supervision session   122
virtual placements   120
Working Together to Safeguard
        Children   96
workplace mentor   8, 10, 26, 30, 42,
        44, 52, 107, 111, 121, 139, 191,
        194
Worsley, A.   26, 123

www.ingramcontent.com/pod-product-compliance
Lightning Source LLC
Chambersburg PA
CBHW070408270326
41926CB00014B/2747